THE MILTONIC SETTING
PAST AND PRESENT

By the same Author

★

MILTON

THE MILTONIC SETTING

SHAKESPEARE'S LAST PLAYS

THE ELIZABETHAN WORLD PICTURE

SHAKESPEARE'S HISTORY PLAYS

POETRY DIRECT AND OBLIQUE

POETRY AND ITS BACKGROUND

THE POETRY OF SIR THOMAS WYATT
(A Selection and a Study)

SHAKESPEARE'S PROBLEM PLAYS

STUDIES IN MILTON

THE ENGLISH EPIC AND ITS BACKGROUND

THE EPIC STRAIN IN THE ENGLISH NOVEL

SOME MYTHICAL ELEMENTS IN ENGLISH
LITERATURE

METAPHYSICALS AND MILTON

Edited by the same Author

ORCHESTRA: A POEM OF DANCING
BY SIR JOHN DAVIES

Chatto and Windus

★

THE HOPE VASES

LAMB'S CRITICISM

THE ENGLISH RENAISSANCE
FACT OR FICTION?

★

With Phyllis B. Tillyard

MILTON, PRIVATE CORRESPONDENCE
AND ACADEMIC EXERCISES

With C. S. Lewis

THE PERSONAL HERESY: A CONTROVERSY

THE
MILTONIC SETTING
PAST & PRESENT

by

E. M. W. TILLYARD

Litt.D., F.B.A.

1961

CHATTO & WINDUS
LONDON

PUBLISHED BY

Chatto & Windus Ltd

LONDON

*

Clarke, Irwin & Company Ltd

TORONTO

FIRST PUBLISHED 1938
SECOND IMPRESSION 1946
THIRD IMPRESSION 1949
FOURTH IMPRESSION 1957
FIFTH IMPRESSION 1961

PRINTED BY THE REPLIKA PROCESS
IN GREAT BRITAIN BY
LUND HUMPHRIES
LONDON · BRADFORD
ALL RIGHTS RESERVED

CONTENTS

PREFACE

In my previous book on Milton, published in 1930, I had little space for his seventeenth-century setting and not much more for his present poetic status. These are now my two main themes; and they are as important to-day as in 1930. It is still necessary to fight the old heresy that Milton was utterly isolated and to insist that he belonged to his age and cannot be understood outside it. Since 1930 a good deal has been written against Milton; but a good deal too in his defence. For instance, Miss Helen Darbishire's introduction to the *Early Lives of Milton* makes out a strong case for the decency of Milton's character (though it did not prevent Mr Belloc from calling Milton a cad and a coward). Miss Rose Macaulay's *Milton*, because it is a fresh study of the poet's life issuing in a sincere appreciation of his poetry, amounts to a serious defence of his high position. Professor Grierson's *Milton and Wordsworth* explicitly defends Milton against recent attack. Mr Desmond MacCarthy has given his testimony; and Mr Charles Williams, in a recent article on the *New Milton*, would relieve him of a number of crimes which even Milton's admirers had hitherto been content to put up with. But there is room for more defences yet. So long as Milton's detractors are vocal, those who value him highly should speak out in his favour, even at the risk of tautology.

I have tried, then, in this book to attach Milton more firmly to his age and to defend him against modern defamation. But my method of defence has been mainly positive. If I have denied what some have said about him, I have tried not to leave a vacuum but to put something in the place of what I repudiate. And in so doing I hope I have contributed something to a new notion of Milton which has been replacing, gradually and even painfully, a no longer wholesome piece of idolatry.

Though both themes are usually present, one or other tends to be more prominent in each section. In my study of *L'Allegro* and *Il Penseroso*, for instance, I am mainly concerned with fixing these poems in their proper setting and with destroying their mythical connection with Horton. In writing of Milton's visual imagination, I am mainly concerned with defending him against a recent attack. In my note on Milton's style I blend the two themes. Anyhow, I hope that both themes are sufficiently sustained to give the unity of a book to a series of chapters which can also be read as separate studies.

In part of my last section I have appeared to stray a long way both from the seventeenth and the twentieth centuries. Study of Milton has led me to that of the epic in general; and I have given, as a necessary prelude to Milton's treatment of the epic tradition, my own interpretation of the course of the epic in England.

One thing I regret. Aiming at brevity, I have had no room to refer to more than a fraction of the recent work on Milton that has interested me. And I should like to apologize for any seeming discourtesy, if I have repeated without comment personal opinions which competent critics of Milton have objected to. I have, for instance, in speaking of *Lycidas*, ignored Professor F. A. Patterson's questioning of the way I read that poem. But my silence in the text of this book must not be taken to mean that I ignore the danger of disagreeing with one so steeped in Miltonic lore as an editor of the Columbia Milton. Among pieces of Milton criticism I should have liked to comment on at length is Mr Empson's *Milton and Bentley* in his *Some Versions of Pastoral*. Knowing that if I once began I should run to a commentary far larger than the provocative original, I have kept myself to a couple of incidental references. But I wish to acknowledge the stimulus I got from Mr Empson. I read with the utmost interest the leading article in the *Times Literary Supplement* of 30 March 1933, entitled *Ormuz and Amurath*. The author, whose name is not known to me, proves Milton's close concern, exceptional among poets of his day, with contemporary exploration in Asia. This concern, which appears first in *Paradise Lost*, shows how in his mature period Milton was absorbed in the particular and in the local even though he merged them in a larger scope. This article reinforces strongly what is one of my main themes in the present volume.

If, now and again, I contradict opinions stated in my previous book, I mean that I have changed these opinions. But I hold with most of what I said in 1930.

My thanks are due for permission to reprint certain studies already published: to the English Association for '*L'Allegro*' *and* '*Il Penseroso*'; to the *Cambridge Review* for *Milton and Prophetic Poetry*, which was a review of a recent book; to the British Academy for the *English Epic Tradition*, which was the Warton Lecture on English Poetry for 1936; to the editors of the volume in honour of Professor Grierson for the *Growth of Milton's Epic Plans*, which appeared under the title of *Milton and the English Epic Tradition*. In all these I have made a few changes, but I have not recast them; and I would ask the reader to bear in mind that I have not tried to disguise the special conditions which influenced the form of the last three. In particular, although the *Growth of Milton's Epic Plans* was written as a sequel to the *English Epic Tradition*, I have preserved the autonomous form into which each study was cast; at the risk (may I warn the reader?) of retaining a few redundancies.

As in my earlier book on Milton, I have tried to combine a certain amount of scholarship with an appeal to the general literary public. It happens that the scholarship is more concentrated in the first and in the two last sections than elsewhere.

For quotations from Milton's verse I have used (with the kind permission of the Oxford University Press) the Oxford edition. If I am blamed for not using the Columbia edition, I would plead that its present high price puts it beyond the reach of most readers. It is more difficult to defend my continuing to refer to the Bohn edition of Milton's prose, when that admirably compact, comprehensive, and serviceable volume, Professor Patterson's *Student's Milton,* is readily available. But, since in England the Bohn edition is still the most widely diffused and the most accessible, I decided to quote from it on grounds of general utility. For quotations from Milton's letters and prolusions I have used my wife's (P. B. Tillyard's) translation.

E. M. W. T.

January 1938

'L'ALLEGRO' AND 'IL PENSEROSO'

The question whether Day or Night is preferable...might seem better suited to a poetical exercise than to a contest of rhetoric.

MILTON, 'First Prolusion'.

Milton, in his character of a Student at Cambridge, sees the Moon terrified as one led astray in the midst of her path thro' heaven.

BLAKE, *describing one of his illustrations of* 'Il Penseroso'.

I

HAYLEY, in his life of Milton, first published in 1794, wrote of *L'Allegro* and *Il Penseroso*, 'it seems probable that these two enchanting pictures of rural life, and of the diversified delights arising from a contemplative mind, were composed at Horton'; and his conjecture has found almost unquestioned acceptance ever since. By their simplicity, their avoidance of politics and religious controversy, their descriptions of rural scenes, they have seemed to fit perfectly into the one period when Milton lived at a long stretch in the country. 'They represent him', wrote Mr John Bailey, 'in his simplest mood, the mood of the quiet years at Horton, spent, more than any other part of his life, in the open air, and among plain folk unlettered and unpolitical.' In these poems at least, people have felt, they can find a Milton who does not disturb them with the qualities they resent in the other poems, a Milton free from the ferocity of *Lycidas*, the heart-searchings of *Paradise Lost*, or the inhospitable bareness of *Paradise Regained*. It has even been possible to throw over them a Rousseauish glamour, to think of them as the reveries into which

Milton fell as he ruminated down the lanes of Buckinghamshire. Pre-eminent in this fashion is the description in Masson's *Life of Milton*, a passage which deserves to be perpetuated as one of the curiosities of Victorian criticism:

Look back, reader, and see him as I do! Now, under the elms on his father's lawn, he listens to the rural hum, and marks the branches as they wave, and the birds as they fly; now, in the garden, he notes the annual series of the plants and the daily blooming of the roses. In his walks in the neighbourhood, also, he observes not only the wayside vegetation, but the whole wide face of the landscape, rich in wood and meadow to the royal towers of Windsor and the bounding line of the low Surrey hills. Over this landscape, changing its livery from day to day, fall the varying seasons....And these seasons have each their occupations. Now the plough is afield; now the sower casts the seed; now the sheep are shorn; now the mower whets his scythe....In summer the twilight steals slowly over the lawn, and, seated at the open window, the poet, who has heard the lark's carol abroad by day, will listen, in the stillness, for the first song of the nightingale; and, when the night is farther advanced, may there not be a walk on the lawn, to observe the trembling tops of the poplars, and to drink, ere the soul is done with that day more, the solemnizing glory of the tranquil stars? Look on, thou glorious youth, at stars and trees, at the beauties of day and the beauties of night, at the changing aspects of the seasons, and at all that the seasons bring! No future years of thy life, perchance, will be so happy and calm as these; and a time comes, at all events, when what thine eye shall have already gathered of nature's facts and appearances must suffice thee for ever, and when, judging thy chambers of imagery sufficiently furnished, God will shut thee in!

Not the scenery alone about Horton, but the little society of the village itself, becomes gradually known to the scrivener's thoughtful son. As he saunters along the road, handsome and fair-haired, the field-labourers and servants touch their hats to him, and think him a little haughty.... Every Sunday, he is one of the little congregation in Horton Church, when all Horton is gathered under his eye; and, as he sits in the pew with his father and mother, and listens to Mr Goodal's sermon, mayhap the presence of the young scholar and critic from Cambridge moves Mr Goodal to a more ingenious strain than need be, and secures for the parish their rector's very best.

I have quoted this as a curiosity and as an instance of how *L'Allegro* and *Il Penseroso* have often been thought of; not to deride Masson's *Life of Milton*. To deride what is at once the best informed and the least informing of all the great literary biographies in English would indeed be easy enough. Masson with his patriarchal manner, his treacly sentiment, and his sabbatical Nonconformity is the very simplest game for modern sophistication. Nor can it be pleaded that he imparts, for all his six enormous volumes, the faintest glow of life to his picture of Milton: his mountain of facts is shapeless and incoherent. And yet Masson was a great man, and, though he has done Milton much harm, not unworthy to be his biographer. His enterprise in undertaking a work on so lavish a scale and his resolution in carrying it out with no abatement of energy and thoroughness to the last page have something of the heroic about them. He never spares himself, exploiting to the utmost every fragment of information that can have the slightest bearing on Milton's life, and in his lavishness throwing in much that cannot possibly have any. He reminds me of nothing so much as of those great Victorian kitchen-ranges, which for all their lamentable waste of coal and heat did somehow succeed in warming the bath-water and loading the dining-table with something which however heavy was certainly food. The last word of any one who has picked up a few crumbs from the feast of Masson should be of gratitude and admiration.

Well, Masson or no Masson, *L'Allegro* and *Il Penseroso* have been very persistently associated with Horton; and superficially the resemblance between the themes of the poems and Milton's country life is plausible enough. But it does not go very deep. Milton had already spent vacations in the country; and there is no specific reference to Buckinghamshire.[1] And in actual fact, *was* Milton mainly occupied in his Horton days with loitering down the hedgerows? Apparently not, for it was at Horton that he settled down to the most concentrated spell of study he ever undertook. To realize Milton's state of mind there, it is necessary to read the prose composition written shortly before he left the University, the *Seventh Academic Exercise*; for it is here that he gives us his own ambitions and the scheme of universal knowledge which he has set himself to pursue. Written not long before he went to Horton, it looks forward, picturing the dominant state of his mind in the years that followed. His theme is the defence of Learning against Ignorance. He begins by

[1] Dr Mackail has said, 'There is nothing in the "scenery" of either poem which suggests Horton as a background, and nothing which is not easily related to Cambridge and its neighbourhood from the "wide-watered shore" of Ely to the "fallows grey" of the uplands and the "tufted trees" of Audley End.'

saying that to be competent in the art of rhetoric—and there can be no mediocrity in rhetoric any more than in poetry—a man must 'acquire a thorough knowledge of all the arts and sciences to form a complete background to his own calling'. And he goes on to complain that his present task has broken in on the studious leisure to which he had settled down. As, in the body of his speech, he surveys the fields of knowledge, he grows intensely excited and betrays the ardour of his own ambitions. There is nothing to compare, he cries, with the joys of Learning:

What a thing it is to grasp the nature of the whole firmament and of its stars, all the movements and changes of the atmosphere, whether it strikes terror into ignorant minds by the majestic roll of thunder or by fiery comets, or whether again it falls softly and gently in showers or dew; then perfectly to understand the shifting winds and all the exhalations and vapours which earth and sea give forth; next to know the hidden virtues of plants and metals and understand the nature and the feelings, if that may be, of every living creature; next the delicate structure of the human body and the art of keeping it in health; and, to crown all, the divine might and power of the soul, and any knowledge we may have gained concerning those beings which we call spirits and genii and daemons. There is an infinite number of subjects besides these, a great part of which might be learnt in less time than it would take to enumerate them all. So at length, gentlemen, when universal learning has once completed its cycle, the spirit of man, no longer confined within this dark prison-house, will reach out far and wide, till it fills the whole world and the space far beyond with the expansion of its divine greatness.

Then he goes on to praise geography and history, history which 'wrests from grudging Fate a kind of retrospective immortality', and ends his survey with a hint of what rewards in private life the truly learned man may obtain:

to be the oracle of many nations, to find one's house regarded as a kind of temple, to be a man whom kings and states invite to come to them, whom men from near and far flock to visit, while to others it is a matter for pride if they have but set eyes on him once. These are the rewards of study, these are the prizes which learning can and often does bestow upon her votaries in private life.

It was the pursuit of these ambitions which had been interrupted and to which at Horton Milton must have returned. Professor J. H. Hanford has shown from his analysis of Milton's notebook that at Horton he settled down, among other things, to a comprehensive study of world history from the original authorities, beginning from the beginning as he conceived it and proceeding in chronological sequence. The conventional picture of the seraphic young 'Lady of Christ's' with his auburn hair, gently admiring the view and yearning over the rustics, must give way to that of a man striving in a concentrated and delighted fury of study to compass the whole circle of human knowledge.

Of course, the more accurate picture of Milton at Horton does not prove that he did *not* write *L'Allegro* and *Il Penseroso* there. It proves that it would not be surprising if he did not write them there. If he did write them there, they are to be considered πάρεργα, not expressing the experiences that mainly held his mind at the time. And such hitherto I have considered them: 'a delightful recreational interlude in the comprehensive studies undertaken at Horton'.

I have, however, never been very happy in my mind about *L'Allegro* and *Il Penseroso*, I mean about where they come in Milton's poetic development. Nor indeed, for all their apparent simplicity, have I been able hitherto to guess what Milton was aiming at when he wrote them. Almost all Milton's early poems were composed for a special occasion, as if he needed some extrinsic persuasion to take him off his main business —even the lines *On Time* were 'set on a clock case': *L'Allegro* and *Il Penseroso* suggest no occasion; without Horton they are in the air, isolated. I now believe there is evidence for relating them to Milton's university days, but before giving it for what it is worth, let me speak of the poems themselves, and of certain difficulties they present.

2

It has been shown that the supposed evidence for connecting the poems and Horton amounts to nothing: first because Milton's main preoccupations at Horton are *not* the main preoccupations of the poems, second because their rusticity would fit equally well with some vacation spent by Milton in the country. Indeed, within the poems there is no evidence for fixing a date: the passages of other authors which Milton undoubtedly imitates or refers to are all too early to affect the issue.[1] Against the poems' belonging to the Horton period is their absence from the Trinity Manuscript,

[1] Professor Grierson, in his introduction to the Florence edition of Milton's poems, cites an analogy with Shirley's masque *The Triumph of Peace*, dated 1634. The analogy seems to me too vague to signify greatly; and even if it did, Shirley might be copying Milton.

in which the undoubted Horton poems occur. It is an inconclusive piece of evidence but not negligible, and it has encouraged Professor Hanford acutely to conjecture that *L'Allegro* and *Il Penseroso* belong to the very beginning of the Horton period or even 'go back to some vacation interval in Milton's university life'. And some years earlier Dr Mackail had made the same conjecture.[1]

And now, what of the poems themselves?

Hence loathed Melancholy
Of *Cerberus*, and blackest midnight born,
In *Stygian* Cave forlorn
'Mongst horrid shapes, and shreiks, and sights unholy,
Find out som uncouth cell,
Where brooding darknes spreads his jealous wings,
And the night-Raven sings;
There under *Ebon* shades, and low-brow'd Rocks,
As ragged as thy Locks,
In dark *Cimmerian* desert ever dwell.

That is the opening of *L'Allegro*, and it is one of the most puzzling passages in the whole of Milton; what possessed him that he should write such bombast? By what strange anticipation did he fall into the manner of the worst kind of eighteenth-century ode? If Milton meant to be noble, he failed dreadfully. If, however, he knew what he was doing, he can only have meant to be funny. And if he meant to be funny, to what end? There is nothing in the rest of the poem that suggests humour—at least of the burlesque sort.

Here, then, at the outset, is a difficulty. But it is isolated, for there is no such obvious shock elsewhere

[1] *Springs of Helicon*, pp. 149–150.

in either *L'Allegro* or *Il Penseroso*. On the contrary, both poems present a superficial simplicity of structure, of thought, and of language. The structure is one of simple progressions and self-evident contrasts; far less intricate than that of *Lycidas* for instance. There is no thought that is not easily grasped at once. Apart from a couple of minor syntactical difficulties the language is extremely lucid. This does not mean that the poems are shallow. Take the couplet

> Hard by, a Cottage chimney smokes,
> From betwixt two aged Okes.

This is simple language, but as poetry the lines are not negligible. We all know that cottage, but the picture we each make is different from our neighbour's. And it is Milton who makes us make our picture. His out-line compels us to fill in the detail. His means—and I doubt whether they can be called simple—are drastic economy of detail and musical suggestion. The heavy beat of the first line has nothing to do with the smoke; it suggests squatness and the quality of being solidly based, in the cottage. Statement and rhythm are doing different jobs of work. The rhythm of the second line rises a little at the end—the oaks are tall—and has something carelessly solid in it—the oaks know their own dignity. (I am well aware of the dangers of talking in this strain; I merely wish to say with some emphasis that the couplet has substance.)

On account of their simplicity the poems give a quick return for any effort expended on them, and hence have attracted a large number of readers. They are the most popular of all Milton's poems. Nor are they the worse on this account. The virtue of good poems with a quick return is very great, in that they convey valuable experiences to those who lack the time or the intellect to grapple with the more difficult. The pity is that there are so few of them, compared with the bad simple poems that produce a swift harvest of fraud.

The mood of the poems is one of an even serenity; not one of the ecstatic serenity that can follow the assuaging of a mental upheaval. They are the work of a young man free for the time from the growing-pains and fevers of youth. We like *L'Allegro* and *Il Penseroso* as we like people when they are happy and tolerant; when they stimulate without exacting too much, do not disturb us by wanting sympathy or by springing fresh notions on us, and are content to enjoy the present. And this analogy easily leads to another quality, best explained in terms of what Dr I. A. Richards in his *Practical Criticism* has called *tone*:

The speaker has ordinarily an attitude to his listener. He chooses and arranges his words differently as his audience varies, in automatic or deliberate recognition of his relations to them. The tone of his utterance reflects his awareness of this relation, his sense of how he stands towards those he is addressing.... Tone, as a distinct character in a poem, is less easy to discuss than the others, and its importance may easily be overlooked. Yet poetry, which has no other very remarkable qualities, may sometimes take very high rank simply because the poet's attitude to his listeners—in view of what he has to say— is so perfect. Gray and Dryden are notable examples. Gray's *Elegy*, indeed, might stand as a supreme instance to show how powerful an exquisitely adjusted tone may be. It would be difficult to maintain that the thought in this poem is either striking or original, or that its feeling is exceptional. It embodies a sequence of reflections and attitudes that under similar conditions arise readily in any contemplative mind. Their character as commonplaces, needless to say, does not make them any less important, and the *Elegy* may usefully remind us that boldness and originality are not necessities for great poetry.

These passages say something that sounds very obvious when once it has been said, but which apparently had not been said and which is extremely helpful. I fancy that *L'Allegro* and *Il Penseroso* are the most popular of Milton's poems because of their subtle friendliness of tone. Some poets deliberately exclude the reader's participation: these are the perversely obscure. Others, though admitting the reader if he likes to participate, do not invite. Others invite—Horace or Goldsmith. Others still, pester—Hugo and Whitman are apt to pester. Others again are coquettish: they pretend to be very aloof, but are really inviting very hard—a romantic vice, to be seen in Byron and the legion of the misunderstood. In *L'Allegro* and *Il Penseroso* Milton displays a perfect social tone. He reduces his idiosyncrasies to a minimum, without at all ceasing to be his characteristic self.

Now this social tone is here connected, as it was in the eighteenth century, with the general and the particular. The eighteenth century disapproved of the personal, the recondite, or the technical, because it thought them anti-social: they could not be enjoyed, as all the parts of poetry should, by all men of taste.

Milton is more generalized in these poems than in any other of his early works. Consider first the case of personal feeling. It is a commonplace that both the Cheerful and the Meditative Man are Milton, and yet there is not the least suspicion that he calls attention to himself. He is no more particularized than the narrator of the *Deserted Village*, nor more important than the shadowy actor who tells the story of *Wuthering Heights*. When he asks Mirth to admit him of her crew, we do not feel that he is trying to exlude others: he is a perfectly well-bred and nebulous Everyman seeking admission to a company whose decorous abstractness would accord with the politest eighteenth-century taste. How prophetic too of the same century are the last lines of *Il Penseroso*, when the Meditative Man utters his hopes of ending his years like a hermit:

> And may at last my weary age
> Find out the peacefull hermitage,
> The Hairy Gown and Mossy Cell,
> Where I may sit and rightly spell
> Of every Star that Heav'n doth shew,
> And every Herb that sips the dew;
> Till old experience do attain
> To somthing like Prophetic strain.

The 'Hairy Gown and Mossy Cell' are quite impersonal, a polite fiction as truly social as their supposed sentiment is anti-social. The eighteenth century was constantly praising the joys and virtues of blameless retirement.

If the supposed speaker is impersonal, most of the

pleasures he enjoys in either of his moods are such as could be shared by any contemporary of decent intelligence and reasonable leisure, and they are uncomplicated by the slightest political or religious controversy. In Milton's youth an educated man was still a musician, and there was nothing either vulgar or recondite about the Fairy Mab.

Not that Milton consistently generalizes. On the contrary, he can vary the general by a flash of the particular; witness the way he describes the shower in *Il Penseroso*:

> Thus night oft see me in thy pale career,
> Till civil-suited Morn appeer,
> Not trickt and frounc't as she was wont,
> With the Attick Boy to hunt,
> But Cherchef't in a comly Cloud,
> While rocking Winds are piping loud,
> Or usher'd with a shower still,
> When the gust hath blown his fill,
> Ending on the russling Leaves,
> With minute drops from off the Eaves.

Here the fancy of the Morn 'Cherchef't in a Cloud', though it would have offended the eighteenth century, was perfectly seemly in the 1630's. The myth of the 'Attick Boy', Cephalus, who forsook Procris to hunt with Eos, told so charmingly by Ovid, is part of the general stock of mythology; it is beautifully set off by the particular observation, the unaffected realism of the 'minute drops from off the Eaves'. The contrast is not quite violent enough to suggest the wit of the Metaphysicals, but it betokens an awakened sensibility. Similarly, in the matter of language, one can compare the quiet generality of

> And who had *Canace* to wife,
> That own'd the vertuous Ring and Glass,
> And of the wondrous Hors of Brass,
> On which the *Tartar* King did ride,

(where Milton in his unobtrusiveness seems to step aside and give place to the actual *Squire's Tale* of Chaucer) with the purely individual 'antick Pillars massy proof'.

Milton, then, in *L'Allegro* and *Il Penseroso*, succeeds largely through his tone. He tactfully and without undue insistence invites his readers to share his experiences. He adjusts his expression to suit his guests, but never so drastically as to obliterate the sense of his own presence.

3

Scholars have not been backward in seeking the literary origins of *L'Allegro* and *Il Penseroso*. Apart from many minor references there are passages that clearly imitate or recall unconsciously poems of Burton, Beaumont and Fletcher, Breton, and Marston. Of these only Burton's poem—*The Author's Abstract of Melancholy* prefixed to the *Anatomy*—has any general bearing. This poem is a dialogue between the pleasing kind and the unpleasing kind of melancholy in the author's brain, and, though this contrast evolves with but small resemblance to Milton's, it is sufficient to have suggested the plan of Milton's poems. But the analogy tells us very little: nothing about the nature of

Milton's poems and nothing about their date. There is, however, another analogy, hitherto undetected, which tells us a great deal more. To put it briefly *L'Allegro* and *Il Penseroso* grew out of Milton's *First Academic Exercise* or *Prolusion*.

Milton's *Prolusions* are exercises in Latin, written from time to time while he was at Cambridge, to fulfil the requirements for getting his degrees. Such exercises were the equivalent—inherited from the Middle Ages—of the modern examination. They were not mere essays, but pleadings in a public debate. The disputant had to be ready to compose his speech in support of either side of the subject at issue, as ordered. Thus in his *Seventh Prolusion*, on the merits of Learning and Ignorance, Milton mentions that he first intended to champion Ignorance but had been requested to change sides. Anyhow, the academic disputation meant a contrast, whether of eulogies or of an attack and a defence.

The *First Prolusion* cannot come later than July 1628, because in it Milton refers to the hostility of the undergraduates to him, which had disappeared by the time he delivered the *Vacation Exercise* or *Sixth Prolusion* at that date. It therefore comes well before any date the critics have assigned to *L'Allegro* and *Il Penseroso*. Concerned with the subject *Whether Day or Night is the more excellent*, it advocates the superior excellence of day. It begins with an elaborate inquiry into the mythical genealogy of Night and Day; goes on to describe the dawning of day and the glory of the sun; and ends by praising day and abusing night. Milton elaborated the mythology in order to display, as it was his business to do, the extent of his classical learning, and to indulge a rather artless and engaging form of burlesque humour. *L'Allegro* and *Il Penseroso* both begin with mythical genealogies, of Mirth and Melancholy respectively, with less elaboration than the *Prolusion* but (in view of other resemblances) in undoubted imitation of it. The mythology finished, *L'Allegro*, like the *Prolusion*, goes on to describe the day-break, and in such similar terms as to leave no doubt that here the *Prolusion* is its original. Here is the prose account:

Even the birds cannot hide their delight, but leave their nests at peep of dawn and noise it abroad from the tree-tops in sweetest song, or darting upwards as near as they may to the Sun, take their flight to welcome the returning day. First of all these the wakeful cock acclaims the sun's coming, and like a herald bids mankind shake off the bonds of sleep and rise and run with joy to greet the new-born day. The kids skip in the meadows, and beasts of every kind leap and gambol in delight. The sad heliotrope, who all night long has gazed toward the east, awaiting her beloved Sun, now smiles and beams at her lover's approach. The marigold too and rose, to add their share to the joy of all, open their petals and shed abroad their perfume, which they have kept for the Sun alone, and would not give to Night, shutting themselves up within their little leaves at fall of evening. And all the other flowers raise their heads, drooping and weighed down with dew, and offer themselves to the Sun, mutely begging him to kiss away the tear-drops which his absence brought. The Earth too decks herself in lovelier robes to honour the Sun's coming, and the clouds, arrayed in garb of every hue, attend the rising god in festive train and long procession.

In *L'Allegro* the lark who sings 'from his watch tower in the Skies' corresponds to the birds in the passage quoted which 'dart upwards as near as they may to the Sun'. And in both the cock is mentioned immediately after the birds. The Cheerful Man,[1] in the poem, comes to the window and bids good morrow to the dawn; in the prose, mankind is bidden to 'shake off the bonds of sleep, and rise and run to greet the new-born day'. Closest of all are the descriptions of the clouds attending the rising sun: compare the last words of the prose passage with

> Wher the great Sun begins his state,
> Rob'd in flames, and Amber light,
> The clouds in thousand Liveries dight.

Later in the *Prolusion* Milton pictures the world's predicament if bereft of day and says:

In vain would the earth bring forth in abundance vines twining in many a winding trail, in vain nobly towering trees.

It may be that

> Through the Sweet-Briar, or the Vine,
> Or the twisted Eglantine,

and

> Boosom'd high in tufted Trees,

echo this.

There remains one important detail of resemblance. The first lines of *L'Allegro*, already quoted and found

[1] If he, and not the lark, is the subject of *com* in line 45 of *L'Allegro*. The corresponding passage in the *Prolusion* might help to settle the question.

so puzzling, are derived from one or two passages in the *First Prolusion*. Here are the most relevant:

Day is the eldest daughter of Heaven, or rather of his Son, begotten by him, it is said, to be the comfort of the race of men and the terror of the infernal god, for fear lest Night should rule unopposed, lest Ghosts and Furies and all that loathsome brood of monsters, unchecked by any barrier between Earth and Hades, should leave the pit of Hell and make their way even to the upper world, and lest wretched Man, enveloped and surrounded by murky darkness, should suffer even in this life the tortures of the damned.

None will you meet save ghosts and spectres, and fearsome goblins who follow in Night's train from the realms below; it is their boast that all night long they rule the earth and share it with mankind. To this end, I think, night sharpens our hearing, that our ears may catch the sooner and our hearts perceive with greater dread the groans of spectres, the screeching of owls and night-birds, and the roaring of lions that prowl in search of prey.

And a little lower down Milton speaks of 'Cimmerian darkness'. The resemblance of these passages to the opening of *L'Allegro* is too strong to need proving in detail; Milton must have had them in mind when he began the poem. Now in their context they are plainly burlesque, especially the second; and it can hardly be doubted that the opening of *L'Allegro* is burlesque also. If so, what was he burlesquing? Immediately, himself. In 1626, when he was seventeen, Milton wrote an ambitious little poem in Latin hexameters on the Gunpowder Plot. He must have concluded that he was trying too much, because he brought it to an abrupt close without recounting the main part of the story in any detail at all. It shows power, but it is crude and bombastic. Milton must very soon have learnt to see its defects. Here is the passage which he may have been parodying in *L'Allegro* and which is certainly behind parts of the *First Prolusion*:

> Est locus aeternâ septus caligine noctis
> Vasta ruinosi quondam fundamina tecti,
> Nunc torvi spelunca Phoni, Prodotaeque bilinguis
> Effera quos uno peperit Discordia partu.
> Hic inter caementa jacent semifractaque saxa,
> Ossa inhumata virûm, et trajecta cadavera ferro;
> His Dolus intortis semper sedet ater ocellis,
> Jurgiaque, et stimulis armata Calumnia fauces,
> Et Furor, atque viae moriendi mille videntur,
> Et Timor, exanguisque locum circumvolat Horror,
> Perpetuoque leves per muta silentia Manes
> Exululant, tellus et sanguine conscia stagnat.[1]

Behind all three places in Milton there is of course a complex of 'horrid' writing, which need not be discussed—Virgil, Seneca, the University Wits, Giles and Phineas Fletcher—and he may be glancing at the whole mode as well as at his immature self. The question *why* Milton should have opened *L'Allegro* with burlesque will have to wait till a much more important likeness between the pair of poems and the *First Prolusion* has been propounded.

[1] 'There is a place hedged in by the eternal gloom of night, once the vast foundation of a ruined abode, now the cave of fierce Murder and double-tongued Treason, whom savage Discord bore at one birth. Here among quarry-stones and broken rocks lie the unburied bones of men and bodies pierced with steel. Here sits dark Fraud for ever with distorted eyes, and Strife, and Calumny, her jaws armed with spikes, and Rage. Here are seen a thousand ways bf death. And Fear and pale Horror flit round the place; and continually the insubstantial ghosts howl through the dumb silence, and the earth in sympathy drips with blood.'

Now an academic disputant had to be ready to support either side of a question set for debate. It is highly probable that Milton had considered what was to be said in favour of night as well as writing his speech in favour of day; that he had the idea of the contrasted eulogy in his mind. Johnson objected to Milton's Cheerful Man and Meditative Man because they were too much alike; and it is perfectly true that they do not supply much contrast to their poems. Nevertheless, the poems *are* sharply contrasted, and the contrast is that between day and night. *L'Allegro* written in praise of day corresponds to the *First Prolusion*; *Il Penseroso* written in praise of night corresponds to what Milton would have said had he been called on to take the other side. The contrast can be worked out in the most precise detail. Melancholy, in *L'Allegro*, is at the opening connected with blackest midnight; Mirth is the daughter of the dawn. Both poems move in a simple progression of time. In *L'Allegro* the progression begins with dawn. The lark startles the *dull* night, and the cock routs retreating night like the stragglers of a defeated army, he 'scatters the rear of darkness thin'. Homage is paid to the source of daylight—'the great Sun begins his state'. The action progresses through the day till in the evening the Cheerful Man carries his cheerfulness into the hostile realms of night by entering the festivities of the town. Hymen carries her taper, and mask and pageantry suggest the light of many candles. *Il Penseroso* is constructed on the same lines, with night and darkness substituted for day and light. The sun is futile, serving merely to show the foolish motes that hover in its beams. Melancholy is dressed in sober black. The progression of time begins with the evening and the nightingale's song. It is to the credit of the embers indoors that they give little light: they counterfeit a gloom. The Meditative Man watches all night and invokes the night ('thus night oft see me in thy pale career'); and when day comes he carries his midnight meditations into the hostile realms of day. Day dawns chastened, hidden in a cloud. 'And when the sun begins to fling his flaring beams' the Meditative Man prolongs night into day by seeking 'twilight groves'. Day is hostile, and he seeks to hide himself from 'Day's garish eie' either by sleep or by taking refuge in the 'dimm religious light' of a cathedral. In fact from first to last the poems are constructed on the contrasted eulogy of day and night.

I hope the case for deriving *L'Allegro* and *Il Penseroso* from the *First Prolusion* has been made convincing. Here is the last piece of evidence. When Milton wrote the *First Prolusion* he had already connected its subject with poetry, for he says:

The question whether Day or Night is preferable is no common theme of discussion, and it is now my duty, the task meted out to me this morning, to probe the subject thoroughly and radically, though it might seem better suited to a poetical exercise than to a contest of rhetoric.

L'Allegro and *Il Penseroso* are the 'poetical exercise' on this theme.

4

If Milton derived the idea of *L'Allegro* and *Il Penseroso* from an oration addressed to a university audience, it is probable that he had a similar audience in mind when he composed the poems. Does such an assumption either explain any of their difficulties, or conspicuously fit any of their characteristics?

One difficulty was the bombast with which *L'Allegro* begins. As it stands, with no background, it is meaningless. There is nothing else like it within the poem to check any conjecture as to its character. It is not organic; and to explain it, extrinsic data are necessary. But an academic audience would not have found it obscure; it would have seen the humour as readily as the Classical Sixth at a Public School would fall to a burlesque of Greek tragedy. Every undergraduate would know Ovid with his endless mythology and would be perfectly familiar with the notion of burlesquing it—even without having read *A Midsummer Night's Dream*. Directly they heard of Melancholy being born of Cerberus and blackest Midnight— infamous coupling—they would have a comfortable sense of familiarity and recognition, and begin to grin. Not only would an academic audience be specially quick to detect the burlesque; it would feel more keenly the force of the opening in the context of the poem. Milton's object is to build up an opening which both in theme and rhythm shall contrast as strikingly as possible with the joy and swing of

But come thou goddess fair and free,

breaking in so suddenly. All readers of course appreciate the contrast—indeed they have found the mere clash of differences so delightful that they have omitted to look closely at one of the colliding bodies. The contrast has been considered merely one of gloom and lethargy with light and movement. But an academic audience would have got more of a shock; it must have had its breath fairly taken away by the sudden swing from the familiar, deliberately dismal melodrama to a joyous and serious beauty. Indeed, I have a slight suspicion of a 'stunt', a suspicion confirmed by Milton's having treated his college audience to things not so very different before. In his *Prolusions* he is very fond of alternating the sublime and the ridiculous, and sometimes does so with a good deal of charm. The most impressive example is when, in the *Sixth Prolusion*, he follows his comic speech with the sublime rhetoric of his *Lines at a Vacation Exercise*. But if a 'stunt', how admirably calculated to delight and impress an undergraduate audience! Indeed, it is only in relation to such an audience that the passage under discussion can be either understood or justified. How it can be understood has been discussed: as the high spirits of a young man it can perhaps be justified.

The social tone of the poems is far more appropriate to Cambridge than to Horton. Milton's last years at college were, with the possible exception of his Italian visit, the period of his early life when such a tone is most to be expected. At first he had not been popular and had thought poorly of his fellows, but by the time of the *Sixth Prolusion*, July 1628, the situation had changed. He says that the old hostility towards him has just changed to friendship and generosity. Moreover, he could not have been invited to take the chief part in so important an affair as this Vacation Exercise had not his talents been appreciated. It is plain that he responded very warmly to the change of opinion and that he was conscious of the social obligations that resulted from it. It is pretty certain that from the summer of 1628 till he took his M.A. in 1632 he was an important person at the University, and that he enjoyed being one. The confidence bred of an appreciative audience and the desire to requite appreciation by considering that audience's likes and dislikes seem to me to be the precise accompaniment to which the airs of *L'Allegro* and *Il Penseroso* are set. And the end of *Il Penseroso*, the prayer for the 'peaceful hermitage' in 'weary age', how charmingly callow, how perfectly appropriate to an audience of boys (one must not forget how young they went to college in those days)! It fits far less well the lips of a man who has retired into studious quiet already. The assumption then that Milton had an academic audience in mind when he wrote *L'Allegro* and *Il Penseroso* seems to me completely justified.

The absence of the poems from the Trinity Manuscript brings with it the question of date. It is in itself but a small piece of evidence in favour of Cambridge rather than Horton: fortified by the discovery that the poems are derived from a university exercise and that they fit a university audience, it becomes a powerful indication that Milton wrote them while still at college. I think it is legitimate to make a close guess at their date. In style they belong to what I have called elsewhere the poems of Milton's early maturity: those less ambitious poems, beginning with the *Song on May Morning*, written after the ambitious failure of *The Passion*. *The Passion* dates probably in Lent 1630. Milton left Cambridge in the summer of 1632. Some date between these two must be sought. In April 1631 the Marchioness of Winchester died, and Milton celebrated her death in octosyllabics. It is highly probable that he continued his essay in that metre with *L'Allegro* and *Il Penseroso*. They are less indebted to contemporary literature than the *Epitaph*, which suggests Jonson and Browne. But Milton had already shown originality in the *Nativity Ode*; there was nothing to prevent a swift maturing after his initial experiment. The *Seventh Prolusion*, already quoted to prove what dominated Milton's mind at Horton, was almost certainly written in his last year at Cambridge. In it he speaks of the studious retirement which had been interrupted, and in the following passage probably refers to a country holiday in the Long Vacation of 1631:

I can myself call to witness the woods and rivers and the beloved village elms, under whose shade I enjoyed such sweet intercourse with the Muses, as I still remember with delight. There I too, amid rural scenes and woodland solitudes, felt that I had enjoyed a season of growth in a life of seclusion.

It is very likely that *L'Allegro* and *Il Penseroso* reflect these woods and rivers and trees and that they are the fruit of that happy season of growth. In brief, they belong to the summer of 1631.

Most readers of Milton will find the above conclusion extremely distasteful; I certainly did myself. To dissociate things so closely and so long linked as *L'Allegro* and Horton is unpleasant, but, the break once made, it should be possible to appreciate the poem more justly, and, by the removal of an impediment, to understand better what Milton was doing at Horton.

A last observation on Milton's addressing his poems to a university audience. That audience mattered much more to him as a poet than has ever been supposed. We shall have to accustom ourselves to associating his poems from *Elegia Prima* (1626) to *L'Allegro* and *Il Penseroso* (1631), his *Prolusions*, and his university audience very closely one with another. Such early Latin poems as the elegies on the Esquire Bedell, the Bishop of Ely, and the Vice-Chancellor are obvious instances of such an association. Had he not been ambitious of impressing his fellows as a poet, Milton would never have inserted his *Lines at a Vacation Exercise* in the comic entertainment he was chosen to give before the entire University. The *Second Prolusion*, on the music of the spheres, imitates or is imitated by a passage in the *Nativity Ode*. The lines *Naturam non pati Senium* were written for one of the dons for public recitation. I have no doubt that any one who troubled to compare the *Prolusions* with Milton's contemporary poems in detail would find many unnoticed connections. I fancy that the request to write *Lycidas* sent to

Milton from Cambridge five years after he went down was due, not to *Arcades* and *Comus*, but to his high reputation as a writer of elegies and other occasional verse while at college. Milton's 'fit audience though few' was a *pis aller*: he wanted as wide a fame as he could get; and at college he seems to have succeeded pretty well. Only, he would never compromise his integrity at any price; fame was never allowed to come first. Milton succeeded in being ambitious without the corruption that often infects ambition.

Postscript. In his important study of the chronology of Milton's early poems (*Review of English Studies*, 1935, pp. 1–8), Mr W. R. Parker confirms the notion that *L'Allegro* and *Il Penseroso* were written in 1631. But see also Professor Merritt Y. Hughes's interesting discussion in his recent edition of Milton (Doubleday, Doran, 1937). Professor Hughes puts 1631 as a tentative date but rightly insists that we cannot say anything more certain than that the poems were written in the later part of Milton's university career. Professor Hughes adds several analogies, including one between the description of the morning in *L'Allegro* and the Latin verses in the Commonplace Book on getting up early and enjoying nature. I should like to correct a false impression my treatment of *Il Penseroso* gave Professor Hughes. He took it that I regarded the whole of *Il Penseroso* as pervaded by an element of irony intended to appeal to the academic audience. But I did not mean that because Milton was aware of his audience, he did not please himself at the same time.

He deals with the kind of things his audience will understand, but he loses himself with all seriousness and without irony in his theme. The youthful touch of the 'peaceful hermitage' in 'weary age' may indeed be, as Professor Hughes says it risks being, a little sentimental, but if so, Milton's youth may excuse a fault not found elsewhere in the poem.

MILTON AND KEATS

MR MIDDLETON MURRY'S *Keats and Shakespeare* is at once the best and the worst book on Keats. No other critic has studied Keats with so fierce a concentration, with such sustained sympathy. Poems, unheeded or slurred over by others, have come alive in Mr Murry's mind; letters, hitherto slackly read, have yielded up to him their immediate significance and their place in the trend of Keats's mental growth. In telling us, then, what was passing in Keats's mind, with what rapidity his powers matured in a short span, and how his poetry kept pace with this growth, Mr Murry speaks with authority. He has proved beyond question that Keats, towards the end of his truncated life, had left the easier 'realm of Flora and old Pan', and that his resolve to pass from it to the 'nobler life' where he 'may find the agonies, the strife of human hearts' had been fulfilled not merely in a few lines of the revised *Hyperion* but in the greatest of the Odes. Keats then emerges an achieved, not merely a potential, great poet.

As long as Mr Murry focuses his vision on Keats alone, all goes well. Unfortunately Keats is made the victim of a larger theory. He is not allowed to develop in his own right; he must be attached to a certain human type of excellence, of which Shakespeare is the most eminent English example. Shakespeare is the Ithaca of Keats's soul-Odyssey; and any competing attractions are in the last resort Sirens, Cyclopses, or

Lotus-Eaters. To such a pitch of excited blindness did Mr Murry work himself up on this subject that he proposed, in a letter to *The Times Literary Supplement*, to emend a perfectly intelligible mention of Timotheus, Alexander's minstrel in Dryden's poem, occurring in one of Keats's letters, into a Shakespearean allusion, 'Tim Ath.' And when he saw in the *Ode to Autumn*, as individual a poem as Keats ever wrote, a re-embodiment of the soul of Shakespeare, he was not much less fantastic.

Besides Shakespeare Milton is a character in Keats's soul-drama. Keats records that he felt the burden of Milton's influence and was plainly relieved to break free of it. Forgetting that no important poet can permanently tolerate the despotic influence of any other poet whatsoever and that Keats had allowed Milton to influence him despotically for a brief time, Mr Murry makes Milton the Cyclops of Keats's Odyssey. Once Keats had escaped, there would be no return to the old bondage. He had passed beyond Milton to a new Shakespearean freedom.

Such theories are at desperate odds with common sense. It is quite plain that any rising poet must find difficulties in coping with any of his great predecessors who attract him. Mr Eliot, in a recent lecture, spoke of the difficulty Shakespeare caused to any modern practitioner of blank verse, how he was an influence to be fought against. If Keats had made *Hyperion* a play instead of an epic and had imitated Shakespeare's dramatic cadences, he would have had to go through just the same process as he did in freeing himself, after the first *Hyperion*, from the Miltonic habits of style. He would have had to escape from a Shakespearean bondage into a new freedom. But it would not have been Shakespeare, any more than it was Milton, who constituted the bondage; the bondage is inherent in the process, inevitable for a growing poet, of passing from reliance on others to a reliance on self. Just before that transition Keats was relying on Milton. A revulsion was inevitable. Can it be doubted, in common sense, that when that revulsion was passed, when Keats had fully felt his own autonomy, he would have returned to Milton for what Milton could give him?

But there is a curious irony in Mr Murry's setting up Milton in opposition to Keats. And it is this: that for a very close likeness with Keats's mental growth we may go to Milton, especially round the time of *Lycidas*.[1] It is a likeness, which, if Mr Murry had read Milton half as carefully as he read Keats, he could not possibly have missed. But from what he says Mr Murry has not penetrated the façade of Milton's rhetoric. For him this rhetoric is a kind of magnificent game, a solemn piece of pageantry, solemn for mere solemnity's sake. Milton's verse he calls something 'constructed by a man of genius in abstraction from the torment of experience'. Strange that the same man can write so ill on one English poet and yet on another write better than anyone else.

[1] Mr Edgell Rickword has written: 'The conscious growth of Milton's genius is certainly not less absorbing to watch than the similar development traced in the letters of Keats.'

In trying to explain resemblances between Milton and Keats, I do not wish either to suggest that they had similar temperaments or that the events of their lives went parallel. On the contrary, Keats's temperament was not very like Milton's and may well have been nearer Shakespeare's; also he matured, in the matter of mental growth though not of poetic technique, much earlier than Milton. On the other hand, they were both very sensitive men, both poets, and as human beings they went the same road. It happens that they recorded certain problems and gave their solutions of them in verse; and the two solutions are pretty much the same. That both poets should act alike when faced with the same crisis unites them more than their differences of temperament keep them apart. Mr Murry really must not be allowed to confine the great generalities of human feeling to the kind of man he happens to prefer; and if Keats's problem and its solution grew out of the 'torment of experience', so too did Milton's.

A minor likeness, not at all obvious at first sight, had better be given before I come to my main one, that between *Lycidas* and the *Ode to a Nightingale*. Of those who have given the best part of their lives to poetry some will have performed a specific mental act of self-dedication. Of these several have recorded that act in poetry. Wordsworth did so long after the event. Keats in *Sleep and Poetry* made the act the theme of his poem. He speaks of

> the deed
> That my own soul has to itself decreed,

and, although full of doubts as to his own worthiness, he will not flinch from his vow:

> What though I am not wealthy in the dower
> Of spanning wisdom; though I do not know
> The shiftings of the mighty winds that blow
> Hither and thither all the changing thoughts
> Of man: though no great minist'ring reason sorts
> Out the dark mysteries of human souls
> To clear conceiving: yet there ever rolls
> A vast idea before me, and I glean
> Therefrom my liberty; thence too I've seen
> The end and aim of Poesy.

Keats's poem, though full of life and promise, is loose, exuberant, and only too explicit in setting forth its theme. For all its many differences, the Miltonic counterpart to *Sleep and Poetry* is the *Nativity Ode*. That this poem bespeaks some sort of youthful excitement is easy to detect. To see within this general excitement the specific excitement of self-dedication would be difficult without extrinsic aid. But from Milton's sixth Latin elegy, in which he refers to Christmas and his writing of the *Nativity Ode*, he speaks so solemnly of the discipline to which the writer of great poetry must submit himself that it is difficult to believe that the motive of personal self-dedication is absent. And if it is present in the elegy, so too is it likely to be in the *Ode*, written at the same time. Such a notion fits that poem's tone perfectly. There is in the hymn 'something neophytic'; there has entered into it 'the serenity that comes from a deep committal, fervently and wholeheartedly made'. And when in the introductory verses Milton urges himself to be before the Wise Men with his poem—

> O run, prevent them with thy humble ode,
> And lay it lowly at his blessed feet;
> Have thou the honour first, thy Lord to greet,
>   And joyn thy voice unto the Angel Quire,
> From out his secret Altar toucht with hallow'd fire—

he sees himself presenting the first-fruits of his new-dedicated muse to Christ, himself, as infant, the first-fruits of the supreme manifestation of the Divine Love.

It is Mr Murry's thesis that during the period of his maturer poetry Keats passed through a fundamental spiritual change; he experienced a species of rebirth; he 'died into life'. As mentioned above, he thinks Milton and Shakespeare had their part in this process. I accept the first part of Mr Murry's thesis, and in what I shall say about Keats I shall be much in his debt. But as for Milton, I believe that he was not at all alien to Keats but that he reveals in *Lycidas* just that process of rebirth Mr Murry attributes to Keats. It marks a crucial passage in the growth of Milton's character and it shows his victorious emergence from the ordeal. Not only are most of the sentiments of *Lycidas* found in the *Ode to a Nightingale* but even the structures of *Lycidas* and of the *Ode to a Nightingale* are almost identical.

If the *Ode to a Nightingale* springs from a mind that has been renewed, it has, too, this mental renewal as its essential subject. It deals with painful things which the poet would fain escape from, which he cannot accept; it ends by the poet's readjusting his old self to those very things and by this very process mitigating their apparently insupportable horror. Pain, sorrow, death; the desire to escape them; acceptance of them in the end; and following it renewed vitality: these are the material of the poem. The particular colour Keats gives this material is of course his own. There is the full Keatsian sensuousness, the intense response to certain primal pleasures, but balancing that, its inevitable concomitant, there is an equal sensitiveness to human suffering. Hence despair and a desire to escape: feelings so powerfully expressed that some readers have allowed them (erroneously, I believe) to dominate the whole poem. But the instinct of life in Keats was too strong: it will not let him escape. The situation is faced and accepted, and through this acceptance comes peace. On the other hand, strong and splendid as his instinct for life is, Keats's characteristic vice, luxury, is not absent. He does somewhat luxuriate, perhaps in pain, certainly in death. This is a general account of the Ode's theme, which will be amplified and illustrated when I describe its structure.

The theme of *Lycidas*[1] can be put in nearly the same terms as those used for the *Ode to a Nightingale*. Death, sorrow, the futility of ambition, the corruption of human nature; the desire to escape them; acceptance of them in the end; and following it renewed vitality. Again Milton colours his material after his own manner. Deeply shaken as he is by the painful and corrupt things he contemplates, he seems funda-

[1] I have dealt with the theme of *Lycidas* in my *Milton*, pp. 79–85, and in my *Poetry Direct and Oblique*, pp. 208–213, to which I refer the reader for more detailed treatment. I cannot here avoid a certain amount of repetition.

mentally more assured than Keats; he does not let his despairing emotions prey on him quite so thoroughly: indeed, he insists on blending with them a measure of dogma and a conscientious sense of literary tradition. The instinct to escape too, though genuinely there, is more of a hypothesis and less of a seriously contemplated possibility than it was for Keats. The renewed vitality, which in Keats remains pure unembodied potentiality, takes on at once the aspect of action; and for him death is not exactly what it is for Keats. Milton is no romantic and cannot luxuriate in it. For him it is to be hated because it cuts short the human activities he so glories in. Like Sarpedon in the *Iliad* he may accept it because after all it heightens life, but not on any other *human* grounds, certainly not as anything self-valuable.

I must now ask readers who have not got the poems by heart to turn to texts of them, while I describe how I think they are constructed.

The *Ode to a Nightingale* consists of two sets of three stanzas, in each of which an assured beginning is partially resolved into a less assured end; a single stanza rising to a solution of the previous doubts; and a coda, of a single stanza, serving not to deny the exalted solution but to allow something not for ever maintainable to ebb into manageable proportions.

The poem's first stanza opens in the full tide of the nightingale's song. Through it the poet has been reduced to numbness, a state expressed with entire conviction through the heavy rhythm of the opening quatrain. But it is no stupid heaviness he suffers, for the rhythm suddenly changes to the other extreme, expressing a rarefied lightness of air. We are in the presence not of coma but of what Keats called indolence. Through his indolent mood he has passed beyond personal pain and sorrow: he does not envy the nightingale, but he is content to rejoice impersonally in the bird's happiness, hence to share in it. This stanza is not only a part of the first movement of the poem, it is also a prelude to the whole; for the rest develops and amplifies the same theme: has the poet really got past envy? can he really be united to the nightingale?

In the second and third stanzas envy returns, for now the bird is out of his reach, in an unattainable region, exempt from the miseries of man. The thought of these is now terribly present. Sorrow is the price of all thought. He must escape. How? Through a drink, an anodyne. Yet the drink is not pure drug and no more, for it was grown in Provence and Helicon, where the Muses lived as well as Bacchus. The instinct to drug himself, to shut out the unpleasant things is there: yet not unqualified.

With the beginning of the second movement (the fourth stanza) there is a sudden rise in energy. The way to join the nightingale is not through Bacchus or an anodyne, but through poetry, which does not blink at the human situation. Then, the union suddenly effected, the surrender having been made, the poem proceeds for a stanza and a half of the serenest beauty, the serenity of nature as Keats describes it symbolizing the serenity of his mood. In the sixth stanza, as in the second and third, the thought becomes complicated and less assured. *Death* here, like the draught of vintage, is equivocal. Partly it is still the death of his own personal hopes and fears leading to a union with the nightingale; partly it is escape once more, and a luxuriating escape—he will evade his responsibilities by dying; partly, perhaps, it expresses a typical romantic sentiment, the desire to perpetuate through death a supreme moment, a desire based on the notion that death is the fixing solution of your emotional snapshot, that if you die now, that *now* is rescued from the flux and becomes eternal. Anyhow, by the end of the sixth stanza the second wave of assurance has been at least partly dissipated.

The seventh stanza gives the solution. That the poet's identification of himself with the nightingale is now perfected is plain from the extraordinary assurance of the rhythm. All thought of escape has vanished. The realm over which the nightingale presides has become one which includes within itself the sorrows of Ruth, the anxieties of kings, and the sufferings of slaves. The poet's regeneration is complete.

In the last stanza the high moment passes. With perfect skill Keats allows the poem gently to fall away. Its sentiment need not worry us. He is not really doubting the validity of his experience; he is merely describing the process of coming to.

Lycidas in its main lines is constructed like the *Ode to a Nightingale*. It is longer and has a more formal opening. After this opening, it is like the *Ode* in having two movements of uncertain issue (lines 25–84 and 85–131). There follows a whole movement whose motive is escape (lines 132–164). This makes a slight difference from the *Ode*, where this motive is diffused through the two first movements. But the rest of *Lycidas*, the solution of the uncertainties in lines 165–185 (the apotheosis of Lycidas) and the falling close of the last eight lines, corresponds perfectly.

The subject of the first movement (lines 25–84) is death. The poet faces and is appalled by death in nature—plague among cattle, canker and frost ruining vegetation—and then by human death. He wishes to escape, and imagines that if the British nymphs had been in their old haunts disaster might have been averted. But he knows the imagining is useless:

> Ay me, I fondly dream!
> Had ye been there—for what could that have don?
> What could the Muse her self that *Orpheus* bore,
> The Muse her self, for her inchanting son?

Death, he goes on, is not merely horrible in itself, it is particularly cruel towards those who have noble ambitions. But he ends on a note of apparent assurance: death of earthly ambitions is made good by heavenly fame. At first sight this movement looks different from the corresponding one in the *Ode to a Nightingale*. There the poet begins with confidence and ends in doubt; here the order is reversed. But actually Milton leaves us rather with a sense of his own anguished and despondent fears lest all the sacrifices he has made for a noble work in this life should be brought to nothing by death. The solution of his fears by the thought of fame in heaven is as yet conventional or incomplete.

The second movement (lines 85–131) repeats, more

or less, the pattern of the first. The poet laments the decay of his times (attaching this subject to Lycidas's death, as the decencies of an elegy required), and ends with an apparent but palpably incomplete solution— vengeance.

The escape motive, absent from the second movement, is the theme of the third (lines 132–164). That Milton knows he is dallying with false surmise does not weaken the poignancy with which he expresses the desire to live in a world better fitted than the one he inhabits, to his heart's imaginings.

The culminating movement, Lycidas's apotheosis, like Keats's seventh stanza, expresses the poet's own regeneration and his reconcilement to life as it is. As human sorrow was included in the nightingale's world, so Lycidas's death, which stands for all the sources of regret found in the poem, is included in the heavenly order described; for he is not merely an inhabitant of heaven but still present on earth, the genius of the shore.

The difference between the two epilogues has already been mentioned. Keats's merely falls away from the high moment, Milton's reinforces the theme of reconcilement. The reconcilement is utter; he can go on his way in the world, ready to deal appropriately with any emergency.

In the first movement of *Lycidas* there are treated or glanced at three themes, either absent from the *Ode to a Nightingale* or not very prominent in it: they are fame or ambition, love, and poetry or authorship. (*Poesy* in the *Ode* is not very definite, perhaps a way of looking at life as well as the act of writing verse.) At love Milton only glances, for at the time of *Lycidas* he was still trying to dispense with it. But poetry and ambition are the qualities by being ready to sacrifice which he 'dies into life'. It is interesting that shortly before the *Ode to a Nightingale* Keats should have devoted a poem to just those three themes found in *Lycidas*: ambition, love, and poetry. For it is personifications of these three abstractions that in the *Ode on Indolence* pass four times before the poet's eyes. The apparently lazy movement and the explicitly lazy sentiment of the *Ode* is remote from the energy of *Lycidas*. Yet the poet reaches the same conclusion. He can do without these absorbing pursuits; he will dare to be indolent, even frivolous for the moment, because such a mood is what his nature now requires. Thus to dare means that he will not sacrifice life as a whole to feelings however urgent or admirable in themselves. Integrity, even when resulting in indolence, must come first:

> So, ye three Ghosts, adieu! Ye cannot raise
> My head cool-bedded in the flowery grass;
> For I would not be dieted with praise,
> A pet-lamb in a sentimental farce!
> Fade softly from my eyes, and be once more
> In masque-like figures on the dreamy urn;
> Farewell! I yet have visions for the night,
> And for the day faint visions there is store;
> Vanish, ye Phantoms! from my idle spright,
> Into the clouds, and never more return!

In *Lycidas* Milton too laid his ghosts; and by the poem he meant: 'Results do not matter, abandon them, lose your life; and you will find yourself.'

As I shall point out in later sections, the general theme that *Lycidas* and the *Ode to a Nightingale* both render is a form of the theme of tragedy. Further comment on it can wait. All that need be added now is that Milton by expressing it very well indeed shows himself as anything but abstracted from the torment of experience. And if the conventional pastoralism of *Lycidas* expresses sentiments so little abstracted, would it not be surprising if the precise theological scheme of *Paradise Lost*, the scholastically balanced debates of *Paradise Regained*, and the rigid neo-classic form of *Samson Agonistes* failed to express the experiences of a living, feeling, and growing mind?

MILTON AND PRIMITIVE FEELING

IF you judged Shakespeare and Milton by the standards of Henry James or Virginia Woolf, there is no doubt that Shakespeare would fare the better. He gives us many more details about the human mind and appears to be more aware of its complications. No wonder, then, if critics like Mr Murry, who insist on judging Milton by Shakespearean standards, find in him a kind of poverty or simplicity. Dr Leavis (who is a better critic when he encourages us to read Carew or Pope than when he puts Spenser or Shelley on the index) finds Milton a very simple soul, a very impoverished sensibility, compared with Shakespeare and Donne. Now it may be that Milton was not a particularly subtle dialectician and that he went to no great pains to refine on his sensations. It is for this reason that discussions on the motives of the persons do not bulk very large in Milton criticism. Whether speaking of his own state of mind or those of his characters, he is content with the large outline. In his reactions to the world around him he seems to have heeded what to him were the bigger issues instead of keeping himself perpetually busy with every size and description of sensuous or intellectual datum. There was no unusual amount of traffic and of breeding among the surface inhabitants of his conscious mind. If the sole object of art were to bring into consciousness, to maintain in an unrelaxed awareness, the daily traffic of an intelligent mind with the world around it, then Milton is not a great artist.

But such a notion is founded solely on what a few carefully selected writers happen to be good at. Judged by actual works throughout the ages it is parochial, and as unjust to the best modern work as to any other. Nor do I believe Dr Leavis holds it except temporarily when speaking of Milton, whom he dislikes. But, Milton having been judged by some such standards, it seems necessary to assert that a sense of greatness in poetry largely depends on the poet's having exploited mental regions other than the surface agitations of the intelligent mind; that Milton exploited them; and consequently that questions of his 'simplicity' are of subordinate importance. More generally, it is timely that those who hold the traditional belief that Milton as a poet had something important to say should restate it in their own manner.

The nineteenth century praised Milton extravagantly: often in terms of inspiration. Because this manner of praise is widely distasteful to-day, we are apt to overlook the perfectly good ground on which much of the praise was founded: a spontaneous and sincere delight in Milton's poetry. For all their outmoded methods the inspirational critics of Milton in the nineteenth century form an impressive body of opinion; they are, if too little critical, yet a cloud of witnesses not lightly dispersed. Others in the Victorian period, the less pious and more articulate, expressed their testimony less by inspiration than by appealing to the passions. Matthew Arnold can speak for them.

Asking himself what actions are most excellent for poetry, he replied:

Those, certainly, which most powerfully appeal to the great primary human affections: to those elementary feelings which subsist permanently in the race, and which are independent of time.... To the elementary part of our nature, to our passions, that which is great and passionate is eternally interesting....A great human action of a thousand years ago is more interesting to it than a smaller human action of today, even though upon the representation of this last the most consummate skill may have been expended, and though it has the advantage of appealing by its modern language, familiar manners, and contemporary allusions, to all our transient feelings and interests. ...Poetical works belong to the domain of our permanent passions: let them interest these, and the voice of all subordinate claims upon them is at once silenced.

Though in this passage from his 1853 Preface Arnold does not mention Milton, he thought so highly of him that he must have included him as satisfying this demand of great poetry. Put thus with its emphasis on the passions, the notion led inevitably to the most successfully passionate of all Milton's characters, Satan. Although I disagree with those who stake the whole value of *Paradise Lost* on him, he cannot but remain a formidable obstacle to those who wish to reduce the poetic stature of Milton. Of the modern Satanists Mr Lascelles Abercrombie is perhaps the most eminent, and a quotation or two from his *Idea of Great Poetry* will express better than I can the still widespread opinion that the character of Satan is of such dimensions that it alone makes Milton one of the greatest poets:

The art of poetry...can do nothing more impressive than the creation of human character. It is never so alive, it never makes such seizure on our minds, as when the result of all its verbal and imaginative technique is our entrance into the life of a character, into a vividly personal form of experience. And so it is with *great* poetry. It is never so great, because never so impressive in its quality of greatness, as when its harmony of some large range of experience comes to life in us in the form of a personal figure.

And of Satan Mr Abercrombie says:

In his character, in the immense consistency of his superbly personal energy, resides the significance of the whole poem; for he is the focus of it all, and out of him and his destiny radiates that mutual relevance of things, which is what we call significance. The whole informing power of the idea, with its wealth of accompanying imagination, and its gamut of emotions, has been concentrated and transmuted into the presence of a living person; and how else could such a profound sense of the basic, the metaphysical contradictions in human existence as Milton's, have been presented in any harmony of impression, unless as the complex harmony of a vast personal life? Here is the very quintessence of individual existence, with all possible pride in its ability to stand out against the mere universality of things....Here...is *Fixt fate—free Will*, the idea of *Paradise Lost*, come to life, and to such a potency of personal life, that it surrounds itself with a world that is one immense tragic harmony—everything that is symbolized by *the Fall of Man*:

> What though the field be lost?
> All is not lost; the unconquerable Will,
> And study of revenge, immortal hate,
> And courage never to submit or yield:
> And what is else not to be overcome:
> That Glory never shall his wrath or might
> Extort from me.

In his insistence on character and in his metaphysical rather than psychological tone, Mr Abercrombie prolongs a nineteenth rather than affects a twentieth-century manner of criticism. The earlier manner may be just as good as the later, but it should not be allowed to remain unsupplemented, if the truth it embodies is to be kept fresh. How then shall one who believes in Milton's greatness put the matter to-day? One contemporary way of referring to great poetry is by different levels of the mind. For instance, if a man thought Milton a greater poet than Donne and was asked to explain why, he would readily find himself saying that Milton, with less surface subtlety and a less feverish interest in the smaller change of thought, has a richer share than Donne of those fundamental qualities of mind that appear to have immediate contact with the forces of life. Such a statement is 'testimony', corresponding to what the Victorians put in terms of inspiration and the passions; and because I want to testify and because a statement of this kind comes readily to me, I shall speak of Milton in terms of different mental levels.

But though perhaps the majority of people to-day who find themselves speaking of Milton's appeal to deep levels of consciousness do no more than put a vague impression of Milton in a vague jargon, there are some who wish, though at great risk, to be more precise about those levels of consciousness expressed in poetry. The risk is great because, of the professional psychologists concerned with the matter, only some care for poetry, and, of those who start from the side of caring for poetry, few are professional psychologists. All the same, however many the pitfalls, I find that a powerful justification of Milton as a great poet, as one whose stature is not affected by questions of intellectual ingenuity or of the simultaneous awareness of four senses to what is going on in the street outside, is to be gathered from what a few people have said about the subliminal content of the most impressive poems.

In his *Varieties of Religious Experience* William James records his personal conviction that

our normal waking consciousness, rational consciousness as we call it, is but one special type of consciousness, whilst all about it, parted from it by the filmiest of screens, there lie potential forms of consciousness entirely different. We may go through life without suspecting their existence; but apply the requisite stimulus, and at a touch they are there in all their completeness, definite types of mentality which probably somewhere have their field of application and adaptation. No account of the universe in its totality can be final which leaves these other forms of consciousness quite disregarded.

And in a neighbouring passage James brings these 'potential forms of consciousness' into relation with art.

Most of us can remember the strangely moving power of passages in certain poems read when we were young, irrational doorways as they were through which the mystery of fact, the wildness and the pang of life, stole into our hearts and thrilled them. The words have now perhaps become mere polished surfaces for us; but lyric poetry and music are alive and significant only in proportion as they fetch these vague vistas of a life continuous with our own, beckoning and inviting, yet ever eluding our pursuit. We are alive or dead to the eternal inner message of the arts according as we have kept or lost this mystical susceptibility.

Here is a principle which surely should be applied to

poetry other than lyric. It is the mark of the greatest poetry that it brings these 'other forms of consciousness' into relation with the form with which we are normally familiar. And no amount of weaving patterns with the latter will be a satisfactory substitute. It is because Milton could pass convincingly from one form of consciousness to another that his alleged 'simplicity' is irrelevant. Thus Milton's description of Paradise in book four of *Paradise Lost* represents one of these 'other forms of consciousness', one of 'these vague vistas of a life continuous with our own'; and he brings it into sharp contrast with normal consciousness, when at the end of the poem Adam and Eve, by now ordinary man and woman, are driven from it to inhabit the world we all know.

However, it is not on the lines suggested by William James that anything at all deserving the epithet 'precise' can be said. On the contrary, he insists on the vagueness of a poetical expression of these 'other forms of consciousness'. For something a little more definite we have to go to writings more anthropological than William James's *Varieties of Religious Experience*. A hint of these is contained in one passage of a lecture not otherwise at all anthropological, A. E. Housman's *Name and Nature of Poetry*. It refers, aptly enough for my purposes, to the line from Milton's *Arcades*, 'Nymphs and shepherds, dance no more'. These words, says A. E. Housman, have their powerful effect 'because they are poetry, and find their way to something in man which is obscure and latent, something older than the present organization of his nature, like the patches of fen which still linger here and there in the drained lands of Cambridgeshire'. Where Housman differs from William James is in insisting on age, on qualities in man inherited from a very remote past. In fact he introduces Milton into that perilous world inhabited by savages and professors with notebooks, and enlivened by taboos, totem-poles, incestuous desires, ghosts, and demons of vegetation. And I agree that Milton has as much right there as most other major poets.

There must be many passing references to the connection of poets with primitive ways of thought. And when such a connection suggests itself spontaneously, it ought to be given consideration as a piece of evidence. Such a connection, having the appearance of spontaneity, I recorded in a recent book.[1] A certain tension of joy and melancholy, found widely in poetry, presented itself to me as something primitive, and perhaps connected with the emergence in remote ages of mankind into self-consciousness. Mr C. S. Lewis seems to be thinking of something primitive when he speaks of Keats's heightened consciousness in a certain passage of poetry being 'something foreign, something won from without, from the boundless ocean of racial, not personal, perception'.

Professor Gilbert Murray is among those who have connected great poetry with certain primitive myths which keep cropping up. These, he says,[2]

---

[1] *Poetry Direct and Oblique*, 1934, pp. 44–52.
[2] In the *Classical Tradition in Poetry*, 1927, lecture on *Hamlet and Orestes*, pp. 238–240.

are deeply implanted in the memory of the race, stamped as it were, upon our physical organism. We have forgotten their faces and their voices; we say that they are strange to us. Yet there is that within us which leaps at the sight of them, a cry of the blood which tells us we have known them always.

He thinks that the susceptibility to such myths is one of the characteristics of the great ages of poetry:

In the greatest ages of literature there seems to be... a power of preserving due proportion between these opposite elements—the expression of boundless primitive emotion and the subtle and delicate representation of life. In plays like *Hamlet* or the *Agamemnon* or the *Electra* we have certainly fine and flexible character-study, a varied and well-wrought story, a full command of the technical instruments of the poet and the dramatist; but we have also, I suspect, a strange, unanalyzed vibration below the surface, an undercurrent of desires and fears and passions, long slumbering yet eternally familiar, which have for thousands of years lain near the root of our most intimate emotions and been wrought into the fabric of our most magical dreams. How far into past ages this stream may reach back, I dare not even surmise; but it seems as if the power of stirring it or moving with it were one of the last secrets of genius.

It is possible to accept this principle as extremely important, without necessarily following Professor Murray through all the intricacies of his myth-hunting. And I believe that Milton possessed eminently this one among 'the last secrets of genius'.

The most elaborate attempt to define primitive modes of thought persisting in poetry is Miss Maud Bodkin's *Archetypal Patterns in Poetry*. Miss Bodkin accepts Professor Murray's position as shown in the

4-2

above quotations and seeks to isolate certain myths or symbols which are rooted in primitive life and which recur in poetry. These myths or symbols she calls 'archetypal patterns' and she believes them to have the power to evoke a peculiarly keen response from the human mind. These patterns have to do with the most universal and unescapable modes of human feeling: the relation of the individual to those parts of his environment common to us all, to his family, to the group in which he finds himself, to events out of his control. They may even typify 'the rhythm characterizing all conscious and organic life'. Such large relations or processes have been conceived in ritual and myth under certain recurring patterns. One of these, according to Miss Bodkin, is the pattern of death and rebirth. This in general symbolizes 'a state of introversion and regression, preceding a kind of rebirth into a new way of life', a rhythm inseparable from all human activity. The death of the tragic hero and the suggestion, which in the greatest tragedy always accompanies it, of resurrection are the typical rendering of this pattern in poetry, though of course they can embody more than this single great generality. Such a rendering remains peculiarly powerful for reasons of age, because we have either inherited its likeness in the structure of our brain or at least because we have that in our brain which is predisposed towards it. To appeal to that predisposition is one of the functions of great poetry, and the ability so to appeal one of the criteria between the great and the small in art. So, too, when the reader responds to an 'archetypal pattern', he undergoes an experience of exceptional force. To quote Miss Bodkin with reference to the general tragic pattern just mentioned:

That poetry in which we re-live the tidal ebb towards death followed by life renewal, affords us a means of increased awareness, and of fuller expression and control, of our own lives in their secret and momentous obedience to universal rhythms.

The above account quite fails to convey the richness and complexity of Miss Bodkin's argument and of the intellectual power and integrity with which it is conducted. All it can do is to indicate the kind of thing she is after. My immediate point is that she finds Milton rich in the expression of archetypal patterns and that, apart from whether one agrees with her finding just those patterns in his poems, she is right in thinking that he owes much of his greatness to being close to primitive and elemental habits of mind and succeeding in expressing that closeness.

The 'patterns' Miss Bodkin discerns in Milton have to do with Heaven and Hell, the recurrent image of woman, and Satan. I refer the reader to her treatment, without comment. Apart from these, I have in my section on Milton and Keats interpreted *Lycidas* as a rendering of the 'rebirth pattern', the pattern of tragedy; and there may be other instances of Milton's power over primitive ways of thought. Let me suggest a couple. Most readers to-day would agree that one of the elements distinguishing an effective from an ineffective account of wild scenery is the power to suggest the feelings of awe which can have been at their height only when man felt the odds of nature against him to be very heavy indeed. The opening of Gray's Pindaric Ode on the *Progress of Poetry* describes wild nature, but what virtues it has are quite unconnected with any primitive fears:

> Awake, Aeolian lyre, awake,
> And give to rapture all thy trembling strings.
> From Helicon's harmonious springs
> A thousand rills their mazy progress take:
> The laughing flowers, that round them blow,
> Drink life and fragrance as they flow.
> Now the rich stream of music winds along
> Deep, majestic, smooth and strong,
> Thro' verdant vales, and Ceres' golden reign:
> Now rowling down the steep amain,
> Headlong, impetuous, see it pour:
> The rocks, and nodding groves rebellow to the roar.

Here the wildness of nature belongs to a pre-arranged pattern, it lives only as a constituent part of a harmony, not at all in its own right. For a contrast one habitually goes to the Romantic poets, but there are passages in Milton that reproduce more instinctively, and with less interposition of theory, than most passages from the Romantics, the primitive awe of wild nature.[1] First, a few lines from the Lady's first speech in *Comus*:

> What might this be? A thousand fantasies
> Begin to throng into my memory
> Of calling shapes, and beckning shadows dire,
> And airy tongues, that syllable men's names
> On Sands, and Shoars, and desert Wildernesses.

[1] Since writing the above I have read Professor Stoll's *Milton a Romantic* (*Review of English Studies*, 1932, pp. 425–436), which points, with much vigour, very much in the same direction. I mention my independence of his article, because the double testimony should carry the greater weight.

Then the last two lines of the passage in which Michael tells Adam the fate of Paradise after the flood:

> Then shall this Mount
> Of Paradise by might of Waves be moovd
> Out of his place, pushd by the horned floud,
> With all his verdure spoil'd, and Trees adrift
> Down the great River to the op'ning Gulf,
> And there take root an Iland salt and bare,
> The haunt of Seales and Orcs, and Sea-mews clang.

All judgments of poetry rest on a series of individual responses. It is not therefore irrelevant to say that these two passages of Milton have for me just that quality of which Professor Murray spoke when discussing the stories of Orestes and Hamlet.

A second primitive feeling may be deduced from the architectonic power which critics have so often praised in Milton. There is something quite uncommon, something alive and passionate in the thorough manner in which Milton shapes and finishes off his plot. Comparisons may put the matter more clearly. The *Prelude* is a solid enough achievement in some ways. The resolution to embed in a single setting those records of passionately felt moments was carried through in a way much to be admired; yet it was devoid of fierceness or exultation, and its carrying through was rather a duty than the source of fresh and independent excitement. Chaucer on the other hand is more like Milton. A small thing like the *Prioress's Tale* is pleased with, while a big thing like the *Miller's Tale* exults in, the completeness of the shaping. Milton's joy in such completeness reminds me of the Q.E.D.'s of Euclid, an analogy not in the least surprising, for Euclid was a person and impressed on the working out of his propositions the exultation of the pioneer succeeding in his exploratory quest. Writing of Milton before I had thought about any connection between him and primitive feelings, I wrote that 'he typifies the controlled energies of the great explorers and inventors. He stands as the perpetual monument of the pioneering spirit in man.' And I should now add that he does so partly through his masterful plot-manipulation; and that the pioneering spirit in man belongs to a phase of primitive man as much as to Galileo and Hudson in Milton's own day. Milton, to express something analogous to the sense of primitive human triumph at having made a new thing with a piece of stone or leather, did not choose Aeschylus's way, that of investing it in a great figure, Prometheus; he reenacted the process through his own craft. As an example, subordinate to the main scheme but complete in itself, take the seventh book of *Paradise Lost*, describing the six days of Creation. Milton's language is here not quite at its best: it is slightly less fresh than in, say, books two and ten; and there are one or two redundancies. But for all that, there is felt the powerful and excited pressure of Milton's effort to *make* the structure aright, to tell the story of Creation in such a way as to lead effectively up to Man, its culmination. And when Man and his dominion are described, the tension breaks and the book issues into the triumph of work well completed, a sensation so elemental as to be shared by the nest-building animals and yet as universal and quotidian as any human sensation whatever. And, when the reader reads this book, he should respond to the primitive emotion in the way Professor Murray describes.

Professor Murray spoke of the need, in the greatest poetry, of combining primitive emotion and the subtle and delicate representation of life. And rightly; because—witness ballad literature—mere primitiveness is not supremely effective. It would seem that for full mental health the channels between the primitive and the sophisticated must be kept open: the traffic should be unimpeded. It is one of the functions of great poetry, by the volume and the freedom of the traffic it reveals, to encourage the reader to keep unimpeded these channels in his own mind. Now it is idle to maintain that Milton fulfilled this function as successfully as Shakespeare, who is equally at home in every portion of the scale and could move with incomparable athleticism up it and down it. But even if Milton is not so athletic, he had sufficient variety to stock a world of much richness, and he can give us the most startling juxtapositions. For instance, after Michael has told Adam of the destiny of Paradise after the Flood, as quoted above, he inserts abruptly one of Milton's most sternly Protestant sentiments, one which is the very antithesis of the superstitions of a primitive life. Paradise was removed, he says,

> To teach thee that God attributes to place
> No sanctitie, if none be thither brought
> By men who there frequent, or therein dwell.

And then Milton encloses this morsel of Protestantism

with another description coming from a very different place in his mind:

> He lookd, and saw the Ark hull on the floud,
> Which now abated, for the Clouds were fled,
> Drivn by a keen North-winde, that blowing drie
> Wrinkl'd the face of Deluge, as decai'd.

If such juxtapositions were very frequent, Milton would be a kind of colossal, unconscious humorist; and they do, when they occur, add a piquancy which is characteristically Miltonic. But they are not very frequent and must not, because they are charming, make us forget the more serious contrasts. It is when Milton's 'archetypal' power is put against such pieces of heightened but normal life as Adam's reconciliation with Eve in book ten of *Paradise Lost* or Samson's lyric lament, 'O that torment should not be confin'd', that his full stature can be understood.

This prolonged dwelling on the primitive may, I fear, be distasteful to some of those who can stomach general references to the unconscious. I shall therefore end more generally. It is possible, too, that everything I have said could be translated into terms of poetic technique; and I suggest that the general platitude I am about to utter is not unrelated to another platitude: that Milton is a very great master of poetic melody. Such mastery implies that he was exceptionally well stored and ordered in the parts of his mind not under the control of his conscious will. And that is a generalization which might be accepted by some to whom traffic with the primitive is repellent. Milton's weakness, as I have noted in writing of *Paradise Lost*, was an imperfect accord between his self as it was and his self as desired by his will; or, to repeat a metaphor, an imperfect clearing of the channels between the primitive and the sophisticated portions of his mind; just as there was a discrepancy between the world as he desired it to be and the world as it was capable of being. All the more astonishing is it that he can have stood the shock of apprehending the discrepancy. The disappointment of his political hopes in one so ingenuously and abandonedly sanguine must have been a shock so vast that only an unconscious exceptionally serene, exceptionally adjusted to the forces of life, could have kept him sane. But in the last resort his fiery, ill-grounded optimism counted for little, balanced by an instinctive deep-seated wisdom. It was this wisdom which found perfect expression in the last lines of *Lycidas* and of *Paradise Lost*, which indeed animates his poetry generally, and which in the end quite mitigates the harm of all surface conflicts.

MILTON AND PROPHETIC POETRY[1]

WITH only one chapter on Wordsworth and that one partly devoted to comparing the ways Milton and Wordsworth took the revolutions of their day, this book is substantially about Milton: a fresh and important estimate of that poet. For writing it Professor Grierson is equipped in certain ways as no one else is. His profound knowledge of the seventeenth century has enriched his understanding without blunting his zest. Unlike the scholar whom Professor Cornford likened to a medlar, he has ripened without going rotten. There is indeed a youthful elasticity about his writing that makes the book a delight to read.

Professor Grierson has one peculiar advantage in writing on Milton. Having edited and praised Donne he cannot be suspected of giving untested allegiance to the old poetic hierarchy of the seventeenth century in which the Metaphysicals were accorded an inferior place. It is this that gives a peculiar force to his defence of Milton against modern defamation. This defence is admirable in itself: coming from the editor of Donne it may penetrate ears which had otherwise been quite sealed up against it. Of Milton's poetic greatness Professor Grierson has no doubt; and if he uses about it words that have been used before, he is yet passing an original judgment, something he has arrived at

[1] *Milton and Wordsworth: Poets and Prophets.* By Sir Herbert J. C. Grierson. Pp. x+185. Cambridge University Press, 1937.

himself from the beginning and not taken over from others.

For another thing Professor Grierson is better equipped than any other writer for dealing with Milton's Protestant theology. It is not easy to keep one's head on this subject—that is if one meddles with it: to ignore it to-day is too ridiculously easy. Till about twenty years ago Milton was regarded generally as a rather narrow and very thoroughgoing Protestant, with a leaning towards the Old Testament interpreted 'fundamentally'. Then the Americans got busy and showed how much he had in common with the classical and stoical doctrines of the Renaissance; while Professor Liljegren carried the notion to an extreme by painting him as a second Machiavelli. Nearer home Saurat put up his fascinating and influential plea for Milton as a daring and unorthodox thinker. Much he said was true; and all lovers of Milton must be deeply grateful to him for doing more than anyone else to destroy the notion of Milton as a fundamentalist who also wrote poetry. Still, when the first effervescence of gratitude subsides, it does become evident that Saurat has made Milton a little too remote from his *total* contemporary setting and a little too close to French anti-clerical rationalism of the late nineteenth century. In other words, both the 'fundamentalisers' and Saurat have been too apt to judge seventeenth-century Protestantism as if it were identical with that of the nineteenth century, hence to distort both it and its effect on Milton. Now of all critics Professor Grierson has shown himself the least prone to that error;

and it is likely that opinion will begin to swing back to his contention that Milton, though in the end of no sect, yet held by the principal tenets of Evangelical Protestantism:[1] a contention made years ago in his article on Milton in *Hastings' Encyclopaedia* and sustained with admirable learning and sensitive understanding in the present book. Not that this change of opinion will turn Milton back again into the narrow theologian he was formerly thought to be; it will rather make us revise our mistaken notions of Protestant theology in the seventeenth century.

The main theme concerns a certain type of poetry which Professor Grierson calls 'prophetic'. There are poets, he holds, who, reaching out to notions beyond the scope of their conscious reasoning faculties, grasp them intuitively and express them in poetic or oracular form. And the notions they grasp are beyond 'the thought and feeling of the society in which they live, the civilization which has shaped their minds and hearts'. On the other hand, they do not merely utter their own private and unique feelings. They have a new message for that society whose thought and feeling they are *not* expressing. They are, then, if I understand Professor Grierson aright, men who are in advance of their age (as we say), groping for something they know not consciously what, and saying it brokenly though impressively and as if burdened with the weight of

[1] It is interesting that Professor Floris Delattre in his clear-sighted and well-balanced introduction to his French translation of *L'Allegro*, *Il Penseroso*, and *Samson Agonistes* (*Collection Bilingue des Classiques Étrangers*, Paris, 1937) is one with Professor Grierson in this matter. See pp. lxxiv–lxxxi.

their message. Such were the Hebrew prophets, struggling away from 'the sensual and cruel nature worship which they saw around them in neighbouring nations and among their own people' to a higher conception of religion. And Professor Grierson thinks that among English writers Blake, Burke, and Carlyle were 'prophetic' in this sense. The present book has for its main theme the question how far Milton was a prophetic poet.

In passing let me point to a matter of critical theory which this 'prophetic poetry' raises. Most writers who put literature in terms of information rather than of states of mind tend to be mystical. They tend to look on poets as men who, through a process of revelation, tell us things about nature or love or what not of which the ordinary person is ignorant. Professor Grierson's doctrine is neither that of the psychologist putting literature in terms of mental equipoise nor of the mystic putting it in terms of revelation. The prophetic poet is anything but a passive vehicle; he does the work himself, but instead of achieving a valuable adjustment of his own mental qualities he, as it were, beats out of his own materials a universally valid human truth, one (at that stage of its development at least) expressible only in poetic or oracular form. Somewhat the same notion of poetry as the vehicle of new ideas is found in Professor Whitehead's *Adventures of Ideas*.

Applying the above criterion to Milton, Professor Grierson finds him up to the beginning of the Revolution essentially the artist and not fraught with any prophetic message. The first great event in his life was the Revolution with all the extravagant hopes it engendered. Milton was dazzled with the vision of an England reformed into a state of pristine apostolic purity and of himself as the prophet-poet of a regenerate England. The rapt utterances of the early anti-episcopal pamphlets are in the true prophetic vein. Milton is striving after something that transcends the reach of his unaided reason: 'can any candid person read such passages...and not feel that they are the words of one stirred to the depth of his soul?' The course of events, however, quickly wrecked the full range of Milton's prophetic ambitions. Disillusioned first by the Presbyterians and finally by the mass of his countrymen, he must commute a national panegyric into a more partisan acclamation of a handful of heroes. Professor Grierson thinks that the final issue of the original prophetic urge is the *Defensio Secunda* with its praise of Cromwell and the other Parliamentary leaders. 'It was not till he had written *Defensio Secunda* (1654) that the idea of a national historical poem was abandoned, as being in a way completed.'

Coming to the three long poems, Professor Grierson does not find in any of them the full prophetic strain. *Paradise Lost* was, in its subject-matter, the product of Milton's reason rather than of his whole mind. Its greatness is artistic. 'Milton as an artist is altogether a larger and more splendid luminary in the poetic heaven than Wordsworth. He is the supreme master of poetic evolution and poetic diction—a style sensuous, impassioned, elaborate, musical, a very cloth of gold.' *Paradise Regained*, too, is an artistic triumph, but in a quite different style. *Samson Agonistes* (with *Lycidas* his most spontaneous poem) is great, less for its prophetic message than for its weight of personal emotion. 'Into no poem has Milton put more of his deepest feeling, his own sufferings physical and mental (but dramatized and so held at a distance), and those haunting doubts about God's ways which had looked out even in his early exultant prose.'

The above account is so simplified that it may be misleading and anyhow it quite fails to do justice to the sanity, the happy gift of illustration, and the many instances of wisdom with which the argument is conducted or reinforced. Better than to specify the book's many merits is to recommend everyone interested in Milton to read it.

It remains now to air some notions which Professor Grierson's treatment of Milton has brought to my mind.

Although I agree that the particular political kind of apocalyptic fervour that animates Milton's early pamphlets is lacking from *Paradise Lost*, I do detect certain parallel activities in the poem, certain ways of feeling with which Milton was burdened and of which he had to deliver himself. Professor Grierson, convinced of the above-mentioned lack, is apt to confine Milton's poetic power to terms of artistry, and in such a way as to suggest for mere artistry a separate existence in which I am sure he is far from believing. In Milton's early poems too he stresses the artistry rather than any 'prophetic' content.

As to the general question, the existence of pure

artistry, I can understand the conception of purely experimental verse, devoid of poetic merit: like Wyatt's worse sonnets. But I cannot understand how any technical innovation to which the reader responds keenly can be made without a corresponding creative act in the mind. If Milton's early poetry was, as Professor Grierson says, that 'of one essentially an artist', it must be something more besides; it must express new and valuable states of mind, of whatever description. That the artistry should be employed on apparently conventional or trite material makes no difference, for the state of mind that counts and gets through may have but a tenuous relation with the poem's professed subjects and have the highest possible degree of originality. Thus Ben Jonson's 'Queen and huntress chaste and fair' is original not only in artistry but in feeling, despite its shamelessly conventional classicism.

Now, if we try to find in Milton's early poems the state of mind of whose existence the artistry is both the pledge and the expression, we shall, I contend, find ways of feeling not too unlike those animating the prophetic outbursts in Milton's earliest pamphlets. Professor Grierson notes how in these Milton's highly strung nature is shaken into rapture by the message that possesses him. But in the early poems too there is both the rapture and the sense of having a message—*some* message, even if as yet he does not quite know what. For the rapture we have Milton's own words, when, writing his Latin Ode to Rouse years after, he records how in meditating his early verse he trod on air—*humum vix tetigit pede*. And, for an actual example (both of the rapture and of the sense of having some message), take the Lady's scholastic dispute with Comus on chastity ('I had not thought to have unlockt my lips'), where the feeling in its vehemence is close to the sublime appeal to God in *Animadversions upon the Remonstrant's Defence* to 'perfect and accomplish thy glorious acts'. Comus, she ends by saying, is not fit to hear himself convinced—

> Yet should I try, the uncontrouled worth
> Of this pure cause would kindle my rap't spirits
> To such a flame of sacred vehemence,
> That dumb things would be mov'd to sympathise,
> And the brute Earth would lend her nerves and shake,
> Till all thy magick structures rear'd so high,
> Were shatter'd into heaps o're thy false heart.

If not actually 'prophetic', that is full of 'prophetic' potentialities.

I think therefore that great as was Milton's exultation in 1641 at the prospect of a reformed England, Professor Grierson is wrong in making the Revolution so sudden and dominating an eminence in the geography of Milton's poetic career.

Further, I fancy that Professor Grierson exaggerates the span of time during which Milton still contemplated a poem founded on his prophetic nationalism in the year 1641. 'I am disposed to think,' he writes, 'though it cannot be proved, that if Milton postponed till as late as 1658 beginning work on *Paradise Lost*, it was because he still dreamed of a great poem dealing directly or symbolically with the liberation of England, the reform of reformation' (p. 71). I cannot myself believe that Milton contemplated putting all his strength into a great national poem after he had come to lose faith in the generality of his countrymen and in the Long Parliament of the years 1646 to 1648. That he did so lose faith is proved by the topical passages that occur in the first four books of the *History of Britain*, books which Milton himself tells us were written in the years before the execution of Charles. Here he inveighs bitterly against the corrupt politicians and divines of the time and deplores the effect these had on the people at large, unfitting them,

now grown worse and more disordinate, to receive or to digest any liberty at all. For stories teach us, that liberty sought out of season, in a corrupt and degenerate age, brought Rome itself to a farther slavery: for liberty hath a sharp and double edge, fit only to be handled by just and virtuous men; to bad and dissolute, it becomes a mischief unwieldy in their hands.

I grant it that the praise Milton bestows on Cromwell and the rest in *Defensio Secunda* fulfilled after a fashion an earlier pledge to exalt the apostles of English liberty, but it points to Milton's reluctance to abandon utterly *any* plan he had made and not to any long-sustained intention to crown his plan with a great poem.

Coming to *Paradise Lost* I find the same difficulty as with the early poems, namely that of seeing it chiefly as a triumph of artistry. Professor Grierson does indeed see more than artistry in many parts of the poem. He pays a fine tribute to the 'strokes of creative and surprising genius' that follow one another in the first four books and to Milton's narrative power. But he allows for no meaning Milton may be conveying extrinsically to the story or to the theological framework. And in so doing he curtails the true scope of the poem. Here is a single instance of the kind of thing he omits.

It was Saurat, I believe, who first pointed out the feeling Milton had for fertility, for exuberant life.[1] It is a simple and very common feeling, but Milton had it with a force quite exceptional even among poets, as if his own teeming brain and soaring temperament were in some intimate way linked with the apparent lavishness of nature in perpetuating the forms of life. The feeling comes out in Comus's extraordinary, crowded account of nature's lavishness,

> Wherefore did Nature powre her bounties forth,
> With such a full and unwithdrawing hand,
> Covering the earth with odours, fruits, and flocks,
> Thronging the Seas with spawn innumerable,

and the rest. It comes out in the heady richness of Milton's imagery in the prose works. But it reaches its full, though ordered and restrained, expansion in *Paradise Lost* alone. There is first the grim, artificial, ironic profusion of Pandemonium; then the supererogatory efflorescence of Paradise, where the flowers were not husbanded after the fashion of earthly gardening but by 'Nature boon'

> Powrd forth profuse on Hill and Dale and Plaine,

[1] See too the excellent development of the same theme in Professor Merritt Y. Hughes's edition of Milton, introduction to Minor Poems, pp. xxx ff. He very justly brings in the first and fifth Latin elegies and even the *Nativity Ode*. He further connects Milton's natural springs of vitality with his frequent descriptions of the eternal world in *Paradise Lost* through figures of dancing: an illuminating and convincing suggestion.

and where the trees 'wept odorous Gumms and Balme'.
Raphael arriving in Paradise passes

> Into the blissful field, through Grove of Myrrhe,
> And flouring Odours, Cassia, Nard, and Balme;
> A Wilderness of sweets; for Nature here
> Wantond as in her prime, and plaid at will
> Her Virgin Fancies, pouring forth more sweet,
> Wilde above rule or art; enormous bliss.

Enormous bliss: all Milton's instincts, not his reason
alone, or his reason combined with his artistry, joined
in distilling that pregnant and perfect phrase. To greet
life, to relish it, to exclaim with Blake 'I want, I want',
was as central a necessity to his nature as it was to
Rubens, that other great neo-classic exuberant of the
seventeenth century. Nor is nature's exuberance confined to the first half of the poem; it is there in the
account of creation, and it is there in that vast geographical catalogue in book eleven describing the
aspect of the earth in terms derived from the great
voyages of exploration or discovery.

This same feeling for fertility appears not only in
the subject-matter but in the very verse-technique of
Paradise Lost. To the construction of Milton's typical
verse-paragraph, that powerfully sustained unit of
rhythm, much artistry must have gone; years perhaps
of meditation and experiment. Yet, unless it is almost
meaningless, it must embody some of Milton's mental
trends. It would of course be conceivable that a man
out of sheer interest in the technical possibilities of
blank verse devised a longer sustained form of it than
had hitherto existed. I can hardly see any admirer of

Milton reducing his motives so low. But, rule out that hypothesis, and the only conclusion is that Milton's verse paragraph was dictated by his inner needs. Those dictating needs must have been many, but one of them was precisely this feeling for fertility which has been illustrated through the actual subject-matter. Bounty is indeed one of the first qualities evident in Milton's verse in *Paradise Lost*. He refuses to measure out his sentences or his rhythms in driblets. He must prolong his sentences with subordinate or participial clauses (even, it must be admitted, to the detriment at times of clarity) till they are ripe to dropping, and he will not relinquish his rhythms till they have worked themselves out to exhaustion and rest,

> secure
> Of surfet where full measure onely bounds
> Excess.

Now this bounty has not a great deal to do with the main theme of *Paradise Lost*, yet it is one of the qualities in Milton's poetry that most promotes his peculiar sublimity. Moreover, it is found at its height in *Paradise Lost*. I conclude that we do that poem serious wrong if we judge it with exclusive reference to its professed main theme.

This bounty or sense of fertility is something too simple and elemental, too remote from the evolution of an idea to be included in Professor Grierson's prophetic poetry. It may indeed be nearer allied to those nature cults against which the prophetic poetry of the Hebrews protested. But at least it sprang from a part of Milton other than the purely ratiocinative (though his reason amply ratified it). He felt the bounty of nature so strongly, he was so permeated with the sense of it that in a way that sense became a burden, a message; and when he delivered that message it was with the consensus and co-operation of all his faculties.

MILTON AND PROTESTANTISM

I WROTE in the previous section of how Professor Grierson has recalled us to the truth that Milton's main doctrines as expressed in *Paradise Lost* were those of Evangelical Protestantism. Even the Arianism, which is explicit in *Christian Doctrine*, he proves to be absent from the poem. True, he ignores Milton's mortalism, the heresy that makes body and soul of one substance, both equally subject to death and subsequent resurrection. But in other respects Milton was orthodox, sufficiently so to be approved and set up as an example by orthodox Protestant divines of the eighteenth and nineteenth centuries. What are we to make of a truth, most unlikely now to be controverted, which more than one popular and influential writer on Milton in recent years has either denied or at least partially evaded?

Why they have evaded it is clear enough. No great proportion of poetry-lovers (in England at least) are enthusiasts for such Evangelical Protestantism as has survived into the twentieth century. More would sympathize (rightly or wrongly) with one of the characters in a novel of Gide, who remarked of a circle of French Protestants that he had never entered into so asphyxiating a moral atmosphere in his life. And in England there might well arise the conviction that at all costs Milton must be saved from the Groups. It has followed that critics have set up Milton the man of the

Renaissance against the traditional notion of Milton the austere Protestant. But in so doing they have made two mistakes. First, they have implied an opposition between the Renaissance and Protestantism which does not exist, one movement being a part of the other. Second, they have seen the Protestantism of Milton's day in a nineteenth-century guise. From such a misconceived version of Protestantism they were quite right to rescue Milton. But they did this good act at the price of fabricating another fallacy: that Milton was not really a Protestant at all. It now behoves us to recognize Milton's Protestantism, to dissociate it from some of our current preconceptions of that doctrine, to try to understand it, and to understand Milton through it.

The above scanty remarks must have given a quite false notion of Evangelical Protestantism to-day; and any adherent of it who may read them has every right to feel indignant. Much of Milton's Protestantism may yet survive; and those who have called Milton no Protestant may have done so partly through ignorance of contemporary Protestant thought. On the other hand it is probable that some of Milton's Protestantism persists in a form that has nothing specifically to do with the Protestant churches, while nineteenth-century Protestantism did throw up excesses and absurdities which Milton would have repudiated. With the hectic and rapturous insistence on the healing power of Jesus's blood which has animated much Evangelical preaching from the time of the Wesleys onwards Milton would have had no sympathy; on the contrary it would have revolted him quite as much as the Catholic doctrine of transubstantiation; while the extreme fundamentalist doctrine (so wittily described by Edmund Gosse in *Father and Son*) that God in creating the world in the year 4004 B.C. deliberately gave it the geological appearance of much greater age in order to try man's faith in the Old Testament, would have appeared to him as barbarous and absurd. On the other hand the *Ascent of F6* by Messrs Auden and Isherwood is quite in the tradition of the Miltonic Protestantism. The hero of that play accepts the full Protestant responsibility of making his own terms with the world, unsheltered and unguided by any set of social conventions; and his sense of sin is of a Protestant unmitigatedness. Years ago Newman said that for good or ill English literature was radically Protestant; nor do I think that the situation has changed since his day. Quite apart from literary merits, the *Ascent of F6* is more centrally English and more traditional than *Murder in the Cathedral* with all its carefully resuscitated Catholic mechanism.

It is of course extremely unfortunate that we have to use the word Protestantism at all in talking of Milton. But we can hardly help it. The reason is that a certain set of impulses, of prime importance in human nature, ever-existing, but fluctuating in their relative power, became for a couple of centuries associated with a certain type of religion. If they were expressed they were expressed typically, *par excellence*, through that religion rather than in another way. Those impulses were in the main the desire of the individual to stand alone and to accept responsibility, and a belittling of all material and adventitious props in exercising this responsibility. The first of these impulses was general to the Renaissance, the second was the specific mark of the most centrally Protestant men, the Puritans.

To-day these impulses are in themselves weaker and they are not particularly associated with Protestantism, while other less exalted motives have been fathered on it. One of these can be called the commercial. Catholic writers (Mr Belloc for instance in his book on Milton) habitually attribute the nefarious habit of usury and even the sins of the modern banking system to the Protestant religion. Mr E. M. Forster, who from his writings appears an agnostic with mystical velleities, in reviewing a book of a pious Evangelical, recalls, with a satisfaction he does not attempt to conceal, the spectacle of the early Victorian industrialist salving his Evangelical conscience by turning over a tithe of his gains from sweated labour to subsidizing missions to the so-called heathen Hindoo; while for the connection of the *petite bourgeoisie* with a hypocritical nonconformity the novels of Mark Rutherford give a picture which in many people's minds excludes any more noble alternative. Milton, with his fierce idealism, his disdain of the petty, of compromise, his improvident marriage with a dowerless girl from a Cavalier family, is as remote from the huckstering side of Nonconformity as a man could be; and it is unfortunate that we should have to characterize him by the word Protestant, which still carries with it so many associations to which he is utterly alien.

Another Protestant failing from which Milton must be kept free is an indifference to external beauty. It must not be thought that Milton, if he could be taken to-day to visit Canterbury Cathedral, would experience any thrill of satisfaction in passing from the catholicizing beauties of the cathedral proper to the beggarly hideousness of the chapel in the crypt that has accommodated the French Protestants since the repeal of the Edict of Nantes. In the pitch-pine pews of Little Bethel Milton would have found no spiritual repose. More likely he would have deprecated worshipping Christ crucified in a building that sins against the Holy Ghost. Nor again, if Milton would be shocked at the casualness and uproar of Mass on a Feast Day in a Catholic church in South Italy, does it mean that his ideal alternative would be a prosperous Wesleyan chapel in Nottingham or Liverpool. A far better idea of Milton's Protestantism can be got by comparing the crowds, the disorder, the mingled reverence and irreverence, the periodic riots and fanaticisms that mark the Church of the Holy Sepulchre at Jerusalem with the intense calm, the luminous spaciousness, the beautiful bareness of a Mahommedan mosque. It is in the latter setting that Milton's Protestantism, his belief in the stripped soul making its peace with God, would best be at home. Or if a pointer is required from contemporary Protestantism itself, a few village churches, that have escaped much restoration, or any touch either of the Simeonite or of the Oxford movements, and have remained bare without being hideous, will give it. There are several such in the Cotswolds, and in the Lake District the church at Hawkshead. With the Protestantism which these embody Milton would have felt a kinship.

My conclusion so far is that we must accept the necessity of calling Milton a Protestant but that we must beware of attributing to him the wrong kind of Protestantism. It remains to estimate the limits of this Protestantism in Milton. For however important it may be, it will not comprehend all the parts of a great poet. For instance it will not have any obvious connection with two Miltonic qualities I have described in the last two sections: his delight in fertility and his kinship with certain primitive ways of feeling. This delight and this kinship are more in the nature of an endowment than of a philosophy. When they are there very strongly and are successfully communicated they may be of high value to the reader. But by themselves they do not impose any pattern on life. Milton's Protestantism has to do with the pattern in which life presented itself to him.

I must here warn the reader that in this last mention of Protestantism I have extended the meaning of the term. Hitherto, when speaking of it in its ideal form, I have confined its meaning to certain impulses which, because of the great emphasis they received, differentiated the reformed religion from medieval Christianity; these I called 'the desire of the individual to stand alone and to accept responsibility, and a belittling of all material and adventitious props in exercising this responsibility'. Plainly those two impulses are too incomplete to constitute a pattern; but they may lead to a pattern. From now onwards I wish the word Protestantism to mean, if need be, the kind of position one can expect such impulses to lead to.

That Milton was swayed by these impulses few would deny, but perhaps I had better mention a little evidence that he was so. For *Comus* to be at all dramatic it was necessary that the Lady should be in genuine peril and temptation; yet the completeness of her isolation argues some motive in Milton's mind other than mere dramatic need. Lost in the dark, deceived by the supposed peasant, still more lost in the alien brilliance of Comus's palace, she is thrown back utterly on her own responsibility. She is indeed rescued by outside help, but not before she had asserted, as completely as a single human being can, her own unalterable conviction. Samson is alone with God. His friends are powerless to help him. For his misfortunes he accepts every shred of responsibility; and it is by that acceptance that he is regenerate. Milton's hostility to the Bishops and to any sequestration of sanctity has the same basis. He would have every Christian his own priest and the individual heart the ultimate altar. In *Reason of Church Government* he states his convictions magnificently. Here is one of several possible passages to illustrate:

But when every good Christian, thoroughly acquainted with all those glorious privileges of sanctification and adoption, which render him more sacred than any dedicated altar or element, shall be restored to his right in the church and not excluded from such place of spiritual government as his Christian abilities and his approved good life in the eye and testimony of the church shall prefer him to, this and nothing sooner will open his eyes to a wise and true valuation of himself (which is so requisite and high a point of Christianity) and will stir him up to walk worthy the honourable and grave employment wherewith God and the church hath dignified him; not fearing lest he should meet with some outward holy thing in religion, which his lay-touch or presence might profane, but lest something unholy from within his own heart should disfigure and profane in himself that priestly unction and clergy-right whereto Christ has entitled him. Then would the congregation of the Lord soon recover the true likeness and visage of what she is indeed, a holy generation, a royal priesthood, a saintly communion, the household and city of God.[1]

For Milton's dislike of aids adventitious to the dignity of man's responsibility there is his description of Adam going out to meet Raphael in Eden:

> Mean while our Primitive great Sire, to meet
> His god-like Guest, walks forth, without more train
> Accompani'd then with his own compleat
> Perfections; in himself was all his state,
> More solemn then the tedious pomp that waits
> On Princes, when thir rich Retinue long
> Of Horses led, and Grooms besmeard with Gold
> Dazles the croud, and sets them all agape.

Milton, then, is emotionally, instinctively at one with the Renaissance exaltation of the individual and with the Protestant desire to return to the supposed primitive simplicities of the Christian religion which allowed of no hindering or mitigating medium between man and God.

Before describing how the above two impulses, so naturally powerful in Milton, created or helped to

[1] Bohn, ii, 496.

create a certain pattern of life, I must mention a quality in him that was bound to limit that pattern. In however varied a guise life presented itself to him, charming or terrifying, simple or bewildering, it was from first to last exceptionally present to him. It was never an insubstantial pageant, and he could never be content with coming to but partial terms with it on the ground that there was another and a better order of things elsewhere. He had to make terms with things as they were.

I am not concerned for the moment with the stages by which Milton was made to apprehend the facts of life. He may have been naïve and slow to apprehend them; he may have been unreasonably Utopian in politics and religion, unreasonably optimistic about the stuff of common human nature: but in the end he came to see with clear eyes the apparent mixture of justice and injustice that marks the scheme of things. In one way life is rigidly just. You cannot get something for nothing; there are no rewards without efforts. Beyond the quickly exhausted legacy of sheer animal well-being we have nothing to spend unless we ourselves put up at least part of a new capital. But well-directed effort is richly rewarded. It is the morality of the *Georgics—iustissima tellus*—and Milton based his active life on it. But against this basic justice of things there is the capriciousness of chance in allowing or not allowing this law to operate. Chance is utterly uneven in manipulating the circumstances allowing men to profit by this law. The anomaly seems to have presented itself to Milton with full force for the first time when he wrote *Lycidas*. Why should Lycidas have died while the ignoble were spared, why should his own labours to live the good life be the potential sport of chance?

As to solutions, it is possible for a man to believe that the capriciousness of chance distorts the basic justice of things so seriously that life in this world is without meaning. As a result he may give up trying to live, or he may stake everything on a dream-world of narcotics or on an imagined future existence; but in each of these choices the method will be to ignore life rather than to assimilate it. Other methods will be through some kind of assimilation. It is possible to hold, for instance, that in spite of the capriciousness of chance, the general law of rewarded effort does hold in the end. However violently nature is impeded, she will in the end reassert herself. Some have seen such a doctrine in Aeschylean and Shakespearean tragedy. Depending as it does on some sort of average, it can only satisfy those whose view of life is strongly social. In moments of group-exaltation a man may well feel that his private case is of little moment and that any injustice it may suffer can merge in the good of the group. Even so the doctrine is more easily held by a man whom life has treated not too badly. However imaginatively sympathetic with the unlucky, he will be better able to think of the average and to accept the total spectacle, if he has not been as it were singled out for the unkindest visitations of chance. If a man has been so singled out or if his feelings are not so strongly social, he may, granted strong courage and vitality, accept the freaks of chance as a challenge and pit his own self against them. If he succeeds in coming to terms with life in his own case, he may postulate for others at least a potential success, however obvious it may be that in fact many have failed. A man, then, may think life bad and try to deaden, to ignore, or to escape it; or he may accept it as on the whole good; or he may accept it for himself and, having done so, be somehow content to allow others to make their own terms. Every normal person will in some degree share all three instincts; they are all within that circuit of the spiritual norm imaginatively comprehensible to every sane person. If therefore one says that the third is that of the Protestant, it is not to deny its universality. Or to put the same thing with a present reference, if we find that Milton held this Protestant view, the width of his poetic appeal may yet remain very great. But it still remains to be seen whether Milton held this view unmodified or unenriched by any other.

However strong a sense Milton may have had of his own individuality, his lack of social sense has been grossly exaggerated. Like most keen relishers of the feast of life, he was not concerned with keeping it to himself. He would have liked to feel himself part, if an important part, of a satisfactory whole. Unfortunately he was a little clumsy in steering himself through life's complexities and did not at first study his fellows closely enough. Hence a number of misfortunes, beginning with his early unpopularity at college. This one however he surmounted, ending his career as something

6-2

of a social figure. Far from being the work of a solitary dreamer, *L'Allegro* and *Il Penseroso* are, as I have tried to show in an earlier section, exceptionally aware of their social setting. Up to the time of *Lycidas* Milton was probably happy, sustained by youth and natural energy. Then, as described above, he was struck with the injustice in the scheme of things. The main theme of *Lycidas* is the poet's regeneration in face of this injustice. His visit to Italy drew him farther out of himself and strengthened his social instincts. He returned, intending to live an ordinary social life, probably to marry, and ready to take his share in what he thought might be the beginning of a new era in human history. In fact he was passionately desirous of accepting life as on the whole good. But he made the mistake of basing his desires not on human nature as it is but on what he hoped it might become through a religious and political revolution or on an ideal he had formed in his own mind. There followed one blow after another. The ideal wife turned out a 'mute and spiritless mate'; the 'new Presbyter' an 'old Priest writ large'; and general human nature too stupid and unaware to take its chances of improvement. God himself seemed to despise his efforts by striking him blind. Having mustered the remains of his hopes with the rise of Cromwell and the defeat of the Presbyterians, he lost them once more at the Restoration.

If at times Milton had been ready to see the order of things as generally good, he must in his worst times have experienced the most desperate desire to escape.

Occasionally, as when in the last book of *Paradise Lost* he describes the world going on

> To good malignant, to bad men benigne,
> Under her own waight groaning,

he seems to betray a profound pessimism.[1] But in *Paradise Lost* his solution of the world's injustice is on a balance the individual and Protestant one. Whatever the fate of the world, Milton does not complain of his own fate; for all his misfortunes it is within his power to create his own mental peace. And if *he* can, presumably, the will being free, others may do the same.

But it would be unjust to Milton to think that he never emerged from that Protestant fortress which was his inviolable refuge in his worst times. He did so in the very act of writing *Lycidas*, and he did so, if with less assurance, after *Paradise Regained*; for something fresh has entered *Samson Agonistes*. I am not one of those who prefer *Samson* to *Paradise Lost*, but I think that it is in *Samson* that we can see the fullest and clearest rendering of Milton's solution of the paradox under discussion. It gives us the average or representative truth about Milton's Protestantism.

Samson, at the opening of the play, although still open to the temptation of despair (like the Red Cross Knight after his rescue by Prince Arthur), has yet achieved his personal integrity. He has purged his pretensions by an utter humility and is content with

---

[1] Professor Grierson thinks that the pessimism here may be no more than a general Protestant characteristic. I still think there is a fresh personal realism in the passage over and above any possible acquiescence in a general contemporary feeling.

his hard lot, however servile. He has no wish to be ransomed by Manoa and would rather earn his bread as a slave at Gaza, thereby preserving some sort of self-respect to the end:

> Now blind, disheartn'd, sham'd, dishonour'd, quell'd,
> To what can I be useful, wherein serve
> My Nation, and the work from Heav'n impos'd,
> But to sit idle on the houshold hearth,
> A burdenous drohe....
> Here rather let me drudge and earn my bread,
> Till vermin or the draff of servil fooa
> Consume me, and oft-invocated death
> Hast'n the welcom end of all my pains.

That is Samson in the Protestant-Stoic citadel; utterly isolated, for his friends are powerless to help him; hard pressed but still unconquered. And if Samson can hold out, and have made his peace with God, why not every man? This puts the situation at its potential worst; yet it need not be so bad, it may actually be much better. But before Milton shows us how it may be so, he puts with incomparable power the paradox of which we are speaking: the justice of things and the appalling vagaries of chance in upsetting the workings of this justice:

> God of our Fathers, what is man!
> That thou towards him with hand so various,
> Or might I say contrarious,
> Temperst thy providence through his short course,
> Not evenly, as thou rul'st
> The Angelic orders and inferiour creatures mute,
> Irrational and brute.

And these vagaries, he goes on, apply particularly to

the righteous, to those who have benefited by the justice of things—

Such as thou hast solemnly elected,
With gifts and graces eminently adorn'd
To some great work, thy glory,
And peoples safety, which in part they effect:
Yet toward these thus dignifi'd, thou oft
Amidst thir highth of noon,
Changest thy countenance, and thy hand with no regard
Of highest favours past
From thee on them, or them to thee of service.

In the end Samson does a supreme act which, without his previous enslavement, would not have been possible, with the final moral that

All is best, though we oft doubt,
What th'unsearchable dispose
Of highest wisdom brings about,
And ever best found in the close.
Oft he seems to hide his face,
But unexpectedly returns
And to his faithful Champion hath in place
Bore witness gloriously.

To many it may seem quite perverse to see in this final moral of *Samson Agonistes* anything but a simple acquiescence in the will of an extrinsic and controlling God, who can be trusted after all, in spite of every appearance to the contrary, to look after the men of his election so that they may be fit for the paradise he has prepared for them. I cannot myself confine the meaning to this precise theological idea. I see in Milton little signs of brooding on another life and every sign of an intense concern with the world as it is. His renewed trust in the highest wisdom indicates some sallying out from the Protestant citadel of the individual self, some renewed faith in the goodness of life as lived now on earth. Samson had, after all, served his country; and the tomb Manoa will raise over him is to be a place of social meeting and an inspiration of others' deeds:

> There will I build him
> A Monument, and plant it round with shade
> Of Laurel ever green, and branching Palm,
> With all his Trophies hung, and Acts enroll'd
> In copious Legend, or sweet Lyric Song.
> Thither shall all the valiant youth resort,
> And from his memory inflame thir breasts
> To matchless valour, and adventures high:
> The Virgins also shall on feastful days
> Visit his Tomb with flowers, only bewailing
> His lot unfortunate in nuptial choice,
> From whence captivity and loss of eyes.

Samson and his misfortunes are merged into the heroic deeds of his whole race: into both his own and those that are to come. The ways of God are just after all: in the end *iustissima tellus* counts for more than the caprices of fate, which at close view seem to overwhelm all else.

To end with so assured a statement would give the false impression that Milton ended an unqualified optimist: a notion about as false as that Shakespeare in his last plays dwelt exclusively 'on the heights'. It would be nearer the truth to put the matter in a vaguer, a more negative way. During Milton's life his various props had failed him in varying degrees: human love, human goodness, human progress. But in the end he regains a potential faith in them and in the earthly order of things. He holds himself ready to act as if he might believe in them. Hence his last pamphlet, the only one he wrote after the Restoration, published two years after *Samson Agonistes*. Thus Milton in the end, though centrally Protestant, spreads out quite beyond the proper and peculiar bounds of the Protestant creed.

MILTON'S VISUAL IMAGINATION

THE occasion of this note is an article by Mr T. S. Eliot on the *Verse of John Milton*,[1] in which he says things about Milton's style which I think mistaken. Were it not for Mr Eliot's great influence as a critic, I should not be provoked to argue. But thinking that he is really likely to mislead a number of people, I add my protest to that already made by Professor Grierson.[2]

I admire Mr Eliot's best criticism so much that I may the better be excused for attacking what I think his worst, that of Milton. It is also possible that unless his worst were so wrong, his best would not be so good. Writing some years ago on the late Sir Edmund Gosse, Mr Eliot said, and quite truly, that he lacked that touch of fierceness that was necessary for the best criticism. Mr Eliot himself has got it. Indeed it is the intense emotional force beneath his would-be dispassionate and judicial air that makes his spare critical essays so impressive. Anyone who feels so strongly runs risks, when he criticizes, of emotional entanglements which the more placid are spared. To such a risk Mr Eliot succumbs when he deals with Milton. So too, but less seriously, when he deals with Shelley. His early remarks on Shelley were so queerly acrid that they proved Mr Eliot's emotions to be involved in some unusual way. Later, he enlightened us by

[1] In *Essays and Studies of the English Association*, xxi.
[2] *Milton and Wordsworth*, p. 125, note 1.

confessing that he had adored Shelley in his 'teens. It is clear that his later dislike of Shelley was in part the dislike of his own adolescence. Mr Eliot still dislikes Shelley as a person, but not in any unusual way; and his latest remarks on his poetry show that the earlier emotional entanglement has been cleared up: the queerly acrid tone has disappeared. But as regards Milton, Mr Eliot's entanglement has not yet been cleared up, and probably will never be. And I should guess that he has hated Milton since first he read him.

I have put things as strongly as this not so much because I disagree generally with Mr Eliot on Milton's style as because to every passage of Milton he quotes by way of illustration he does some grave injustice. The cumulative weight of this injustice suggests an unusual impediment in his mind. I give two examples. First a comment on a passage from *Lycidas*:

> Whether beyond the stormy *Hebrides*,
> Where thou perhaps under the whelming tide
> Visit'st the bottom of the monstrous world;
> Or whether thou to our moist vows deny'd,
> Sleep'st by the fable of *Bellerus* old,
> Where the great vision of the guarded Mount
> Looks toward *Namancos* and *Bayona's* hold.

Mr Eliot says this is a passage 'than which, for the single effect of grandeur of sound, there is nothing finer in poetry'. Taken in its context this comment can only mean that the lines are pre-eminent for grandeur of sound and for nothing else. It seems therefore that Mr Eliot has failed to see one of Milton's most obvious and powerful displays of the visionary imagination: the image of the Archangel Michael, guardian of the mount named after him, looking over the sea with unimpeded view to Finisterre on the north-west coast of Spain. The only difficulty in sharing Milton's image is that it depends on a piece of geographical knowledge: namely that Namancos is the district of Finisterre and that there is no land between it and Land's End in Cornwall. But Namancos and Bayona were marked on several atlases in Milton's day; and since the beginning of last century all annotated editions give the gist of what we want. Anyhow, without the image of the Archangel in its proper setting the passage lacks quite half of its force.

The second example is a comment on a passage from *Paradise Lost*. Here Mr Eliot not only ignores much of the sense of the passage but (and not for the only time in his article) the context in which it occurs. He writes:

I can enjoy the roll of

> ...Cambulu, seat of Cathaian Can
> And Samarchand by Oxus, Temir's throne,
> To Paquin of Sinaean Kings, and thence
> To Agra and Lahore of great Mogul
> Down to the golden Chersonese, or where
> The Persian in Ecbatan sate, or since
> In Hispahan, or where the Russian Ksar
> In Mosco, or the Sultan in Bizance,
> Turchestan-born...

and the rest of it, but I feel that this is not serious poetry occupied about its business, but rather a solemn game.

The passage occurs in book eleven of *Paradise Lost* (lines 388 ff.), where the context is that Michael intends giving Adam a survey of the whole world and a synopsis of all history; and, in view of the poem's proportions, in a comparatively confined span. Milton's immediate business is to give the reader the impression of great spaces of the earth and great epochs of history —to do so succinctly is quite necessary to the scheme of the poem—and he does it by using his great musical powers to get across a necessarily abbreviated enumeration. Yet for all the brevity every name or place mentioned is strictly associated, and should be associated, with a great event in history or some place made famous by the accounts of travellers. And they all have to be perpended to the full. Mr Eliot writes as if Marco Polo and Camoens had never existed or aroused men's interests; and the levity he imputes to Milton is precisely his own in reading the passage as he does.

To come to the gist of Mr Eliot's essay, he is convinced of Milton's greatness but confines it to that musical power already overstressed by the late Victorians. Milton's senses, he thinks, were not generally active; and his blindness was of prime importance because it confirmed a deficiency of visual sensitiveness and a hypertrophy of aural sensitiveness. 'At no period is the visual imagination conspicuous in Milton's poetry.' Milton cannot convey the 'feeling of being in a particular place at a particular time'; and such pictures as he does create tend to be general.

Mr Eliot seems to connect sensuous vitality with the effect of particularity, but I think without reason. Some sorts of sensuous excitement stimulate people to vague and generalized expression. Swinburne, for instance, could hardly be called deficient in sensuous vitality, even if he was not very discriminating, but I should not call his poetry 'particular' in Mr Eliot's sense. So, too, common sense, a shrewd judgment of human nature, and active emotions may give particularity without the aid of any unusual sensuous power, witness Swift or Jane Austen:

> Behold the fatal Day arrive!
> How is the Dean? He's just alive.
> Now the departing Prayer is read:
> He hardly breathes. The Dean is dead.
> Before the Passing-Bell begun,
> The News thro' half the Town has run.
> O, may we all for Death prepare!
> What has he left? And who's his Heir?

This is good verse, particular enough but hardly sensuous at all. I prefer therefore to keep the two topics separate; and I begin with the topic of the general and the particular in Milton.

Mr Eliot's assumption that it is necessarily better to imply the particular place and time in poetry is natural enough and is also pretty widely made. It is natural, because it corresponds with the method of living modern verse; and those who practise a certain method are prone to think, because it is valid for them, it must be valid for everyone else. For examples of the particular and the general consider these two pieces of verse, one a poem called *Gipsy* by D. H. Lawrence, the other a passage from one of Spenser's *Four Hymns*. They both concern the power of love over the lover:

> I, the man with the red scarf,
> Will give thee what I have, this last week's earnings.
> Take them, and buy thee a silver ring
> And wed me, to ease my yearnings.

For the rest, when thou art wedded
   I'll wet my brow for thee
With sweat, I'll enter a house for thy sake,
   Thou shalt shut doors on me.

The last line is certainly a very localized and particularized way of saying that the gipsy is willing to surrender his most cherished possession, outdoor liberty. Spenser, on the other hand, is vague and general in statement, or, if particular, in a conventional and bookish way:

Then forth he casts in his unquiet thought,
What he may do, her favour to obtain;
What brave exploit, what perill hardly wrought,
What puissant conquest, what adventurous pain,
May please her best, and grace unto him gain;
He dreads no danger, nor misfortune feares,
His faith, his fortune, in his breast he beares.

Thou art his god, thou art his mightie guyde,
Thou, being blind, letst him not see his feares,
But carriest him to that which he had eyde,
Through seas, through flames, through thousand
    swords and speares;
Ne ought so strong that may his force withstand,
With which thou armest his resistlesse hand.

Witnesse Leander in the Euxine waves,
And stout Aeneas in the Troiane fyre,
Achilles preassing through the Phrygian glaives,
And Orpheus, daring to provoke the yre
Of damned fiends, to get his love retyre;
For both through heaven and hell thou makest way,
To win them worship which to thee obay.

Most moderns attempting to write like that would make themselves ridiculous; but that does not mean that the passage lacks either beauty or force, or that for certain purposes the general may not be effective.

There is another modern tendency that makes for an insistence on the particular: that of judging all other English poets by the standards of Shakespeare. It is in itself dangerous because like the Bible Shakespeare will always yield to the seeker what he has made up his mind he wishes to find. Apart from this Shakespeare was a dramatist, and drama tends to be more particularized than, say, the ode or the philosophical poem. If then a relatively high proportion of Shakespeare's verse tends to the particular, it is no reason why particularity should be exacted from all poetry. Had Shakespeare chosen a non-dramatic form, the balance of general and particular might have been different.

On the other hand, if a poet is so generalized that he is incapable of ever giving 'the feeling of being in a particular place at a particular time', he will be the narrower in range, a weaker poet. Mr Eliot seems to think Milton limited in this way, very great but confined. Actually Milton has both methods at his command and uses them as the inner necessity of his experience dictates. The end of *Paradise Lost*, for instance, is as particular as anything can be; in *Paradise Regained* the wilderness is made as little like an earthly wilderness as possible. This is not because Milton could not have dramatized it into something like the heath in *King Lear*, but because the dramatic was the last thing he wanted. For a mixture of general and particular within a short space there are *L'Allegro* and *Il Penseroso*. Mr Eliot says that the imagery[1] of

---

[1] By 'imagery' Mr Eliot in this essay means the scenes presented or descriptive power, not the total metaphorical content.

these two poems is 'all general', and he quotes the six lines beginning 'While the ploughman...'. They are indeed somewhat generalized in effect (though they would have been more so if Milton had not made his ploughman whistle); and that because Milton intends just here to sketch the general country scene the cheerful man might walk through on many days of the year. Elsewhere in the two poems it suits him to be particular:

> Or if the Ayr will not permit
> Som still removed place will fit,
> Where glowing Embers through the room
> Teach light to counterfeit a gloom,
> Far from all resort of mirth,
> Save the Cricket on the hearth,
> Or the Belmans drousie charm,
> To bless the dores from nightly harm.

Sir Arthur Quiller-Couch speaks of Shakespeare's power of reinforcing the general by the particular and illustrates by the line from *As You Like It*:

> And unregarded age, in corners thrown.

Milton in this passage does precisely the same. The 'still removed place' is general, but the lines that follow localize and characterize it, till we are 'in a particular place at a particular time'. A few lines farther down he describes a shower in the early morning. Beginning with a polite mythological reference to Eos and the 'Attick Boy', he ends with the acute particularity of the 'minute drops from off the Eaves', when the shower is over.

Nor is it in the least just to say that Milton grew progressively less a master of the particular or that his blindness impelled him towards the general. Nothing could be more rigidly and concentratedly particularized than parts of *Samson Agonistes*:

> Ask for this great Deliverer now, and find him
> Eyeless in *Gaza* at the Mill with slaves—

these lines particularize the time and place not only in professed sense but in their effect on the reader's imagination.

In short, Milton uses both general and particular with such variety that to try to tie him down to a short formula is to invite disaster.

Secondly, there is the question of Milton's sensuous power. Mr Eliot thinks Milton deficient in sensuous appreciation and hence in all-round richness of metaphorical content. Now though I think him wrong in denying Milton a sufficiency of sensuous appreciation he may be pointing towards a truth, namely that Milton was never content to rest in the senses and to express his deeper experiences in simple terms of them. The poem where Milton is most sensuous is *Comus*; and passage after passage could be quoted from it to disprove the charge of sensuous poverty. One must suffice:

> Unmuffle ye faint stars, and thou fair Moon
> That wontst to love the travailers benizon,
> Stoop thy pale visage through an amber cloud,
> And disinherit *Chaos*, that raigns here
> In double night of darknes, and of shades;
> Or if your influence be quite damm'd up
> With black usurping mists, som gentle taper
> Though a rush Candle from the wicker hole
> Of som clay habitation visit us
> With thy long levell'd rule of streaming light,
> And thou shalt be our star of *Arcady*.

The penultimate line in particular shows a sensuous awareness (and in addition a vividness of the visual imagination) as powerful as can be found in any poet. But *Comus*, however good it is and although no one but Milton could have written it, does not represent the norm of his style. A predominance of direct and simple sensuousness did not in the end fit what he had to express; and though he never lost his mastery of it, or stopped using it, his later general trend was to use the mental picture or the recollected picture or no precise picture at all rather than the immediate sensuous perception, in expressing his experiences. The picture of the Archangel Michael looking over the sea from his mount with uninterrupted view towards Spain is a gigantic piece of visual imagery but it has not the immediate sensuous quality of the 'long levell'd rule of streaming light'; it is a composite of several recollections or imaginings not the reproduction of something seen and intensely apprehended in every-day life. And *on the whole* it is more characteristic of Milton. But this method vastly gains in power, because there is always in Milton the reassurance that the simply sensuous picture was within his grasp. For a second example take the account of the angels discarding their arms and throwing mountains on their opponents in the sixth book of *Paradise Lost*:

> Thir Arms away they threw, and to the Hills
> (For Earth hath this variety from Heav'n
> Of pleasure situate in Hill and Dale)
> Light as the Lightning glimps they ran, they flew,
> From thir foundations loosning to and fro
> They pluckt the seated Hills with all thir load,

7-2

Rocks, Waters, Woods, and by the shaggie tops
Up lifting bore them in thir hands: Amaze
Be sure, and terrour seis'd the rebel Host,
When coming towards them so dread they saw
The bottom of the Mountains upward turn'd,
Till on those cursed Engins triple-row
They saw them whelmd, and all their confidence
Under the weight of Mountains buried deep,
Themselves invaded next, and on thir heads
Main Promontories flung, which in the Air,
Came shadowing, and opprest whole Legions arm'd.

It was an uncommon and very powerful visionary sense that pictured the mountains, complete with woods and springs, torn up and falling root-foremost on the devils' artillery, but the total picture is remote from the immediately sensuous. Yet this imagined, this fabricated picture, reminding of a great baroque painting, is as it were vouched for by a touch of the sensuous. The word *shadowing* in the last line provides it. Not only does it tell us that the flying promontories were so large that they darkened the sky; it implies that their shadows could be seen moving over the landscape, with an immediate evocation of the common sight of cloud-shadows, on a day of sun and wind, racing across the earth.

Sometimes (and he seems to have made a deliberate practice of this in his last two poems) Milton works his richest effects with little sensuous appeal and almost without metaphor. I take as example a passage from *Samson Agonistes* which Mr Eliot cites with approval and which yet he does injustice to:

> The Sun to me is dark
> And silent as the Moon,
> When she deserts the night
> Hid in her vacant interlunar cave.

Mr Eliot gives this as an example of Milton's failure to 'infuse new life into the word'. He thinks 'interlunar' a stroke of genius but that it is 'merely combined with "vacant" and "cave", rather than giving and receiving life from them'. On the contrary, it is by the new life Milton infuses into words mostly familiar, yet without the use of any vivid picture or metaphor, that he gets a most powerful effect. No English poet, I believe, had ever called the sun silent, and the conjunction of the two words is not only new but has a dramatic relevance to the blind speaker. In the monotony of his blindness he must, to be expressive, do more than reiterate the fact of darkness; so he translates the visual *dark* into the aural *silent*. A caviller might object that Milton stole the sun's silence from the first canto of the *Inferno*:

> tal mi fece la bestia senza pace,
> che, venendomi incontro, a poco a poco
> mi ripingeva là dove il sol tace.

But he gives the notion quite another point by putting it in the mouth of a blind man. And, anyhow, would it be decent for Mr Eliot of all men to object to a poet's lifting two words from Dante? 'Vacant interlunar cave' works through a great charge of relevant meaning co-operating with an appropriateness of sound. Of the three words, 'cave' has least weight. It suggests barrenness, but it is there partly because the ancients supposed the moon to retire into one during the intervals of her appearance, and it was well bred to repeat their supposition. (I am not excluding other reasons, but I don't think the word will carry a very heavy load of meaning.) Quite otherwise, however, with 'vacant'. I suspect that Mr Eliot allows it no more meaning than the plain 'empty' and that he thinks it merely repeats part of the idea of 'cave': in other words that it is no more than a bit of padding with a nice sound, lulling us pleasantly over two syllables till we get to the real meat of the passage in *interlunar*. But that is not what *vacant* means: it means 'where the moon is in vacation, where she has nothing to do and can't get on with her proper job of lighting the world'. It is Samson's own anguish that dictates the word, for Samson is thinking of his own 'vacancy', his own utter impotence of doing those things for which he is best fitted. With such a charge of meaning 'vacant' does more than lead up to 'interlunar'; it insists on sharing the emphasis with it. And the two words interact. The chill remoteness, the utter inhumanity of 'interlunar' quench the human appetencies implied by 'vacant'. Milton then is using and using successfully a method as far removed as possible (as regards simple sensuousness) from the passage from *Comus* with which I began.

Once again it must not be thought that Milton ever lost his power over the simply sensuous. A few lines after the passage just quoted Samson says,

> Why was the sight
> To such a tender ball as th'eye confin'd,
> So obvious and so easie to be quench't,
> And not as feeling through all parts diffus'd,
> That she might look at will through every pore?

This is the very height of sensuousness, the body conscious of itself with its own consciousness. D. H. Lawrence might have said that the solar plexus rather than the head created the last line. For the suggestion of delicate sense of touch nothing could excel the third line of these three, likewise from *Samson Agonistes*,

> Dire inflammation which no cooling herb
> Or medcinal liquor can asswage,
> Nor breath of Vernal Air from snowy *Alp*.

To revert now to Milton's frequent habit of getting away from the simply sensuous, it must be realized that to blame him for doing as he did implies much more than that he is unsatisfactory as a poet. It implies a condemnation of a widespread habit of mind. There have always been people who will not quite submit to the terms of life as they find them and who cannot but try to do something about the matter. When they are poets, they chafe at the limits of the five senses and base part of their visions on their composite imaginings and not on their simple sensuous impressions. Hence Blake at an early age is impelled to write

> Like a fiend in a cloud
> With howling woe....

Moreover every great poet will share in some degree this idealizing tendency. For instance when Shakespeare writes of the 'cloud-capp'd towers, the gorgeous palaces, the solemn temples', he creates a composite, recollected picture, quite as remote from sensuous immediacy, quite as idealizing as anything in Milton. Had he written on the theme of *Paradise Lost*, he would have used that kind of picture more frequently than he does in any of his plays. And what he is doing in that passage from the *Tempest* represents a large human impulse it is desperate to condemn.

I will end with quoting a passage from Coleridge's *Table Talk*.[1] In it the great critic not only avoids the deplorable habit, mentioned above, of judging Milton by the standards of Shakespeare but says things about Milton's imagination which are appropriate to the present discussion:

The Imagination modifies images, and gives unity to variety; it sees all things in one, *il più nell' uno*. There is the epic imagination, the perfection of which is in Milton; and the dramatic, of which Shakespeare is the absolute master. The first gives unity by throwing back into the distance; as after the magnificent approach of the Messiah to battle, the poet, by one touch from himself—

　　—'far off their coming shone!'—

makes the whole one image. And so at the conclusion of the appearance of the entranced angels, in which every sort of image from all the regions of earth and air is introduced to diversify and illustrate,—the reader is brought back to the single image by—

　　'He call'd so loud that all the hollow deep
　　Of Hell resounded.'

The dramatic imagination does not throw back, but brings close; it stamps all nature with one, and that its own, meaning, as in Lear throughout.

[1] Coleridge's *Miscellaneous Criticism*, ed. Raysor, 1936, p. 436.

A NOTE ON MILTON'S STYLE

A STUDY of Milton's style would need a book to itself, while for a summary treatment he would be a rash person who thought to better Walter Raleigh in the last two chapters of his *Milton*. All I aspire to do in the present section is to question certain objections that have been levelled with some persistence against the style of Milton's mature poems. These objections are not confined to those who would belittle Milton's poetic stature. The late Mr Francis Birrell, for instance, though holding Milton our second poet, yet wrote of him:

For 200 years Milton has been the schoolmaster of English poetry, and a worse schoolmaster could in some ways hardly be imagined; for, in obedience to his temperament, he twisted diction and prosody into shapes for which they were never intended. Dryden saw this, and would have nothing to do with them.

(Who, one may ask, God excepted, can say into what shapes diction and prosody were intended to be cast?) Another admirer of Milton, the late Mr T. Earle Welby, wrote of Milton's mature poems:

They are beyond description magnificent, but they are the arterio-sclerosis of English poetry. Its impulses are denied to the blood; there is very little of the 'negative capability' which Keats noted in Shakespeare, though there is an almost incomparable art of 'stationing' the deliberately selected fact. We are in the presence of things most wonderfully made, but not of things miraculously born. Milton had almost done with miraculous births when he wrote, at twenty-one, the 'Nativity Ode'.

The mention of Keats and Shakespeare along with Milton suggests that Mr Welby had been reading Mr Murry's book, which in its turn goes back to Keats himself for some of its opinions on Milton. It may be simpler then to begin with Keats, especially as his words on Milton have often been torn from their context and sometimes misinterpreted.

From Keats's letters it is clear that the three English poets he valued most highly were Shakespeare, Milton, and Wordsworth. It is a mistake to think that he worshipped Milton with an ill-considered adolescent idolatry and that he then outgrew him. His admiration was never idolatrous. Before he fell under the influence of Miltonic blank verse, he had compared Milton and Wordsworth as philosophers, quite coolly. He said he was uncertain

whether Milton's apparently less anxiety for Humanity proceeds from his seeing further or no than Wordsworth: and whether Wordsworth has in truth epic passion, and martyrs himself to the human heart, the main region of his song.

In the end he concludes Wordsworth the better philosopher, not because he is personally Milton's superior, but because philosophy has advanced generally since Milton's day. The 'march of mind' (that bugbear of Peacock) has been proceeding. Anyhow, there is no question of Keats's being in any way enslaved by Milton.

About the time of the first *Hyperion* Keats certainly read deeply in Milton, but not exclusively. He did not put Milton up against other poets. 'Shakespeare and the Paradise Lost every day become greater wonders to me. I look upon fine Phrases like a Lover.' Mr Murry, relying, it is true, partly on what Keats later said about 'Miltonics', would have it that Keats's Miltonic period, when he was writing the first *Hyperion*, was artificial and inorganic, and that he escaped from it into a Shakespearean freedom. This 'looking upon fine Phrases like a Lover' would imply a delight in fine phrases for their own sake, and an art that consisted in creating deliberately such phrases. Possibly, but why make Milton responsible when Keats mentions Shakespeare along with *Paradise Lost*? Keats wrote those words at a period when he was developing rapidly, when he was ready to renounce any specific imitative debt to any predecessor. It happened that he had chosen to exercise his strength on a narrative poem, for which form a Miltonic tinge was usual. Had he exercised his strength just then on a Shakespearean sonnet-sequence instead, he must have reacted to 'Shakespeareans' precisely as he did to 'Miltonics'. He must have passed from a way of writing not quite organic, partially derivative in style, to a way wholly his own. That in the two following passages Milton figures as the object against which he reacts is therefore something of an accident, just as it was an accident that Keats fell under Leigh Hunt's sway (rather than under some other contemporary's) and had to free himself from it. Referring to his own *Ode to Autumn* he wrote:

I always somehow associate Chatterton with autumn. He is the purest writer in the English Language. He has no French idiom, or particles like Chaucer—'tis genuine English Idiom in English Words. I have given up Hyperion—there were too many Miltonic inversions in it—Miltonic verse cannot be written but in an artful or rather artist's humour. I wish to give myself up to other sensations. English ought to be kept up. [21 September 1819.]

Here it is plain enough that Keats has done with Miltonizing. But there is no suggestion that Keats objected to Milton's style for Milton. Further, Keats has taken up with a theory of 'pure' English and has set up Chatterton's diction against that both of Milton and of Chaucer. Mr Murry, anxious at all costs to establish his thesis, cuts out Chaucer and substitutes Shakespeare for Chatterton. Of course if you wish to discredit Milton by an antithesis, you are far more effective if you set up Shakespeare against Milton, than if you set up Chatterton against Milton and Chaucer. Only it happened to be the latter antithesis that Keats presented; and I can see no reason for not considering it. But before saying more, let me give Keats's second passage on Miltonics and Chatterton, written actually on the same day. Speaking of foreign poetry he has been reading, he wrote:

I shall never become attached to a foreign idiom so as to put it into my writings. The Paradise Lost though so fine in itself is a corruption of our Language—it should be kept as it is unique—a curiosity—a beautiful and grand Curiosity. The most remarkable Production of the world. A northern dialect accommodating itself to Greek and Latin inversions and intonations. The purest English —or what ought to be the purest—is Chatterton's. The language had existed long enough to be entirely uncorrupted of Chaucer's gallicisms, and still the old words are used. Chatterton's language is entirely northern. I prefer the native music of it to Milton's cut by feet. I have but lately stood on my guard against Milton. Life to him would be death to me. Miltonic verse cannot be written but in the vein of art—I wish to devote myself to another sensation.

What emerges for certain from this rather strange passage? Above all that Keats has done with Miltonics; and he is thankful to have got over that phase of subordination. Yet Milton remains great as ever. On the other hand, Keats is hostile to the language of *Paradise Lost*, with which he associates the gallicisms of Chaucer; and again he sets up Chatterton as a model. Of the critics who have quoted Keats as condemning Milton's language, how many, I am tempted to ask, have mentioned that he condemned Chaucer's too, or that this condemnation was part of a theory of language with which Chatterton was connected? If we want to discover what Keats meant by his remarks on Milton, we had better consider his remarks on Chaucer and Chatterton at the same time.

Chaucer's well of English, far from being undefiled, was, in Keats's opinion, tainted by gallicisms; on the assumption that 'pure' English is as 'northern' a 'dialect' as possible. Milton was like Chaucer in departing from this northern linguistic ideal; only the fault imputed to him is not that of vocabulary but of word-order. Keats seemed also to think that Milton's prosody was not northern but, presumably, classical, since he describes it as 'cut by feet'. In the year 1819, when Keats wrote, it would hardly be possible for an educated man to believe that the Rowley poems were an authentic fifteenth-century document; so, when he says of Chatterton's verse that 'the language had existed long enough to be entirely uncorrupted of Chaucer's gallicisms, and still the old words are used', he can only be thinking of the originals from which Chatterton drew his archaistic dialect. Those originals Keats took to be works of a later date than Chaucer, in fact of the fifteenth century. Briefly, then, Keats's theory of English poetic diction on 21 September 1819, when he wrote the two passages under discussion, was that English looked to a nordic ideal of purity, that Chaucer (with whom English proper begins) fell short of it through his gallicisms, that this ideal was realized in the fifteenth century, that Milton fell short of it through his southern inversions, and that Chatterton realized it once again shortly before Keats's own day. Those who are in the habit of taking the whole of Keats's correspondence with deep and consistent gravity will be forced to associate his sentiments with the nordic excesses of Dr Furnival and Professor Freeman and to expose him to a quite considerable charge of nonsense. A little acquaintance with Lydgate, Occleve, and Skelton is enough to deprive the fifteenth century of any supposed nordic purity of language, while to abstain from great latinization has been a habit of some poets in most ages. As to Keats's notion of Chatterton's 'purity', this from the *Bristowe Tragedie* would satisfy almost any standards of pure English:

Thenne came the maior and eldermenne,
  Ynne clothe of scarlett deck't;
And theyre attendyng menne echone,
  Lyke Easterne princes trickt:

And after them a multitude
  Of citizenns dydd thronge;
The wyndowes were alle fulle of heddes,
  As hee dydd passe alonge.

And whenne he came to the hyghe crosse,
  Syr Charles dydd turne and saie,
'O Thou, that savest manne fromme synne,
  Washe mye soule clean thys daie.'

But Chatterton did not always write so simply and so
little archaistically. When he most imitates archaic
diction and affects archaic manners, he is 'pure' only
according to nordic pedantry, not according to the
common sense of general opinion:

'Tys songe bie mynstrelles, that yn auntyent tym,
Whan Reasonn hylt herselfe in cloudes of nyghte,
The preeste delyvered alle the lege yn rhym;
Lyche peyncted tyltynge speares to please the syghte,
The whyche yn yttes felle use doe make moke dere,
Syke dyd theire auncyante lee deftlie delyghte the eare.

Perchance yn Vyrtues gare rhym mote bee thenne,
Butte efte nowe flyeth to the odher syde;
In hallie preeste apperes the ribandes penne,
Inne lithie moncke apperes the barronnes pryde:
But rhym wythe somme, as nedere widhowt teethe,
Make pleasaunce to the sense, botte maie do lyttel scathe.
                    (*Epistle to Mastre Canynge.*)

Taking Keats's statements with full gravity, we are
forced to believe he committed the absurdity of
thinking such writing 'pure'.

  Keats's nordic theory prompted another statement
that can only be called absurd: that Chatterton's

prosody was native, while Milton's was not. He prefers the 'native music' of Chatterton to 'Milton's cut by feet', and speaks of the 'Greek and Latin intonations' in Milton's verse. The antithesis is utterly false. It is only such experiments as those of Sidney, Spenser, and Campion, or of Robert Bridges, in quantitative metres, that can be said to be 'cut by feet'. Milton's prosody is English. The rhythms of Latin prose and verse have indeed exercised a powerful modifying influence on much English writing, as for instance those of the Vulgate on the English Bible. But that is an influence so wide, subtle, and diffuse that we cannot gauge its limits. Indeed, it is highly probable that Chatterton himself was not ultimately unaffected by them. The three verses quoted from the *Bristowe Tragedie* are rhythmically of the eighteenth century: they are excellent contemporary ballad metre. Now the practitioners of that metre were men versed in Virgil, Horace, and Cicero: and it is very likely that they transferred something of the sonority of these Latins to their handling of their English metres. And if they did, Chatterton inherited at least a fraction of that sonority.

It is, indeed, far more sensible not to take all Keats's letters with equal gravity, and in particular to take the passages under discussion with not the utmost degree of seriousness. Removing the microscope and using the common human vision, we should not find it hard to see the trend of Keats's thought. Ambitious and conscious of his own maturing powers, Keats attempted an epic. Both because he admired Milton and because much of the narrative verse before him had been Miltonic, he allows his style at times to take on a Miltonic tinge. For some reason, probably because he is not yet old enough, he cannot sustain the epic pitch, and throws his work over, and with it the Miltonic style he has been using. Part of his motive in finishing with Miltonics is a desire for independence, praiseworthy and inevitable in any great poet when he is growing up. Now the only kind of poetic independence that is usually undesirable is independence of contemporary literary habit: the contemporary yoke can be accepted with no feeling of servitude. However archaistic, Chatterton is a late eighteenth-century poet, and at the same time one of those least tied to what was most moribund in the verse of that century. Reading Chatterton after Milton, after any poet of an earlier date, Keats must have felt the kind of freedom and affinity that only contemporary verse can give. To him, as a verse-writer (not as a reader), Chatterton was life; Chaucer, Milton (or Shakespeare for that matter) were death. It was good for Milton to write Miltonically ('life to him') but not for Keats or anyone else in the year 1819 ('death to me').

As to Keats's magnificent aphorism that 'English ought to be kept up', I fear once again that we must not allow it to bear too great a burden of meaning. Of course it *should* mean that the language must develop and yet must maintain its essential genius. But I greatly suspect that we must take the nordic context into account and that it means rather '*English* ought to be kept up', or that we must stick to Saxon words and throw out the frenchified or classical interlopers: a much more confined and less agreeable significance. Keats in fact is giving his blessing not only to the 'wyndowes fulle of heddes' of Chatterton, but to the same author's 'lithie moncke' and 'lyttel scathe'. And if this is so, we shall be doing Keats no kindness if we here insist on taking him so very seriously. Better to think of his sentiments as quite fugitive suggestions.

I have written at such length of these passages in Keats's letters because I believe they have sanctified (through misinterpretation) many false judgments on Milton's style. If that sanctification turns out to be unjustified, the judgments to which I refer may carry less weight.

Of one fallacy I speak with some hesitation, especially as I have been guilty of it myself: I mean the habit of condemning Milton out of hand as a specific object of poetic imitation. Of this I quoted an example from Mr Birrell when he said that no worse schoolmaster of English poetry than Milton could be imagined. I am not especially attracted by the Miltonizing blank verse of the eighteenth century, but if I read it more assiduously I might like it better. So might others who have said hard things of it. And it may well be that, conditioned as it was, eighteenth-century poetry did well to model itself in part on Milton. Anyhow, I have not the slightest faith that by refusing to imitate Milton it would have developed powers that it now does not possess. However, this is not a topic I wish to pursue, and I will content myself with asking those who have condemned eighteenth-century Miltonics without having given the matter a great deal of attention to read (or to re-read) Dr C. V. Deane's *Aspects of eighteenth century Nature Poetry*, before they reiterate their condemnation.

I pass now to the two major charges against Milton's style. They have both been implied or stated in the passages already quoted in this section. The first is that Milton's style hardened into a remote grandeur, forsaking the common English speech and the common feelings of men, becoming in Mr Welby's words the 'arterio-sclerosis of English poetry'. The second is that Milton's poetic method was inorganic, that he clothed prose notions in a magnificent poetic dress rather than conceived notion and clothing in a single act of the imagination. Mr Welby called his art the '"stationing" the deliberately selected fact'. And Mr Eliot repeats the charge when he considers Milton in a certain speech to be introducing a deliberate complication into what was a previously simplified and abstract thought.

Taking the first charge first, I will begin with three considerations which we should bear in mind when we read Milton's later poems. The first is what I might call the principle of reassurance, a literary principle to which more prominence might well be given. I was first made aware of this principle by a remark made by Professor D. S. Robertson in a lecture on Homer. Why is it, he asked, that Homer, though dealing with war and a small aristocratic society, yet makes us feel that he includes the complete experience of all kinds of men in the *Iliad*? It is through the reassurance conveyed by a few passages, casually referring to

8-2

humble people (camp-followers and the like) or to the smaller activities of peace. Because of these passages we are assured that Homer knew all about those many sides of life which, through the kind of theme he had chosen, he was compelled almost entirely to omit.

Turning to Milton, I would say that we are only too apt not to apply this principle of reassurance to *Paradise Lost* (and I plead guilty of this omission myself). Finding in the *Nativity Ode* a pervasive tenderness, or in *Comus* a crowded opulence of sensuous feeling, and missing these qualities from the norm of Milton's style in *Paradise Lost*, we too hastily assume that Milton as he grew up had lost them altogether. I am now disposed to agree with Mr Blunden that *Paradise Regained* gives us (among other things) the perfection of the 'Doric delicacy' attributed by Wotton to Milton's early verse and to see many small hints in *Paradise Lost* arguing that neither Milton's homeliness nor his tenderness nor his sensuousness had atrophied in that poem. Nowhere are such hints more evident than at the end of the poem; and if they appear at the end, is it likely that what they tell of has been lacking throughout?

> So spake our Mother *Eve*, and *Adam* heard
> Well pleas'd, but answer'd not; for now too nigh
> Th' Archangel stood, and from the other Hill
> To thir fixt Station, all in bright array
> The Cherubim descended; on the ground
> Gliding meteorous, as Ev'ning Mist
> Ris'n from a River o're the marish glides,
> And gathers ground fast at the Labourers heel
> Homeward returning.

Here at this crucial moment of the poem, in the last lines which cannot but stand for much that the poet has been wishing to convey, comes the homely image, fixed in Milton's brain probably in childhood, of the evening mist creeping from the river and the peasant returning to his home. At another high moment, the end of the first book, Milton reassures us that he has not discarded the delight in peasant superstition that has charmed readers of *L'Allegro*. He compares the devils who shrink themselves into dwarfs to

> Faerie Elves,
> Whose midnight Revels, by a Forrest side
> Or Fountain some belated Peasant sees,
> Or dreams he sees, while over head the Moon
> Sits Arbitress, and neerer to the Earth
> Wheels her pale course, they on thir mirth and dance
> Intent, with jocund Music charm his ear;
> At once with joy and fear his heart rebounds.

Sensitive to the new standards of truth that were arising during the seventeenth century, Milton must needs slip in 'or dreams he sees'. But there is no evidence in this passage of any conflict between a piece of the early, romantic, Milton that has anachronistically lingered on in spite of himself and the supposedly austere Puritan of his middle age. On the contrary, the passage should reassure us that the Milton of *Paradise Lost* assimilated as well as went beyond the early Milton who loved the fairy lore of Puck and Queen Mab. Mr Charles Williams, in an admirable article,[1]

---

[1] *The New Milton* in *London Mercury*, July 1937, pp. 255–261. On *Paradise Lost* as summing up Milton's previous experience see Miss Rose Macaulay, *Milton*, pp. 121–126.

has pointed out how wrong readers have been in imagining that Milton opened *Paradise Lost* with an 'organ prelude'. He points out how much of the young Milton still remains in the later work.

The austere Milton, sonorously sounding the august art of his verse, has been generally made to begin with an organ prelude. But the opening is much more like softness than sonority; it is almost shy. 'The Lady of Christ's' possessed still, so many years afterwards, a kind of maidenly modesty in beginning his high task. That humility, the lack of which causes such laughter in heaven and such misapprehension of the facts in hell, is present in the first twenty-six lines of invocation. The Muse and the Spirit are not commanded but implored.

As a final instance of reassurance (out of many others that might be found) I take Milton's occasional excursions into striking, or unusual, or vernacular diction in his later poems. No one, in view of his prose, is now likely to deny to Milton a Falstaffian opulence of vocabulary; but the fallacy that he damaged himself by straitening it in *Paradise Lost* is quite widely spread. It is perfectly true that Milton (sensitive once more to the trend of advanced opinion in his own day) reacted against the riot of verbiage that makes the Elizabethans and Jacobeans so exhilarating. Instead, he tried to extract the utmost of significance from simple words like *fair* or *joy* or *strive*. Yet in so doing he did not impair his powers, for every now and then he breaks out into that Elizabethan opulence that had marked *Comus*, reassuring us that it has been there in its fullness, though he has not chosen to use it all the time. Nor are these reassurances confined to the early books,

usually considered richer in vitality than the later.
Take these words of God the Father in book ten
describing how he has intentionally prompted Death
and Sin, his hell-hounds, to prey upon the world:

I call'd and drew them thither
My Hell-hounds, to lick up the draff and filth
Which mans polluting Sin with taint hath shed
On what was pure, till cramm'd and gorg'd, nigh burst
With suckt and glutted offal, at one sling
Of thy victorious Arm, well-pleasing Son,
Both *Sin*, and *Death*, and yawning *Grave* at last
Through *Chaos* hurld, obstruct the mouth of Hell
For ever, and seal up his ravenous Jawes.

If Milton made that kind of writing the exception in
Paradise Lost it was by choice not through any poverty
or inhibition.

The second consideration we should have in mind
when we read Milton's later poems is the demand
made on any poet of the mid-seventeenth century by
current critical theory. When a modern critic com-
plains that Milton did not write *Paradise Lost* in the
style of Shakespeare, he is doing something which the
whole critical opinion of the Elizabethan and Stuart
epochs would have utterly repudiated. It was one of
the fundamental principles of Renaissance and neo-
classic criticism that different literary styles were
appropriate to different literary forms. When, for
instance, Spenser wrote an eclogue on the homely
allegory of the oak and the briar, he put it, as was
expected of him, in a homely guise. To satire and
epistles a not too heightened style was thought fit. An
epic written in a conversational style would have been

an outrage. The seventeenth-century theory of stylistic propriety is illustrated neatly enough in Dryden's remarks on the different styles of the epic and the epistle in his Preface to *Religio Laici*:

If any one be so lamentable a Critique as to require the Smoothness, the Numbers, and the Turn of Heroique Poetry in this Poem; I must tell him, that, if he has not read *Horace*, I have studied him, and hope the style of his Epistles is not ill imitated here. The Expressions of a Poem designed purely for Instruction ought to be Plain and Natural, and yet Majestic: for here the Poet is presumed to be a kind of Law-giver, and those three qualities which I have nam'd are proper to the Legislative style.

Such being the contemporary theory, you can complain of Milton's having forsaken the tone of ordinary talk only at the price of demanding of him that he should have shocked the dearest opinions of his time. In other words you imply not only an attack on Milton, but that monstrous folly, an indictment of a whole epoch. You are condemning simultaneously the tragic style of Racine, and the pictorial style of Poussin and Claude Lorraine. And the wider theory on which attacks on Milton's style are based, that there is an orthodoxy of keeping close to common speech, would exclude from grace a large part of the world's literature. For instance, most oriental poetry and the whole of Italian poetry from Petrarch to Carducci are written in an artificial language remote from common talk. The Latin hexameter was in its very essence an imposition on the accentual rhythms of the popular verse. What is to become of Lucretius and Virgil?

Now Milton, far from being isolated from contemporary opinion, was acutely sensitive to it. He was no whit more a rebel against the literary demands of his age than was Shakespeare. Much of Davenant's Preface to *Gondibert* might almost have been written by Milton himself. For his allegiance to the doctrine of the appropriate style consider his first poem on Hobson. It is a humorous but kindly epitaph on a homely person; and for it Milton uses the language, word-order, and broken rhythm of common speech, because he thought that style to be appropriate.

> Here lies old Hobson, Death hath broke his girt,
> And here alas, hath laid him in the dirt,
> Or els the ways being foul, twenty to one,
> He's here stuck in a slough, and overthrown.
> 'Twas such a shifter, that if truth were known,
> Death was half glad when he had got him down;
> For he had any time this ten yeers full,
> Dodg'd with him, betwixt *Cambridge* and the Bull.

Here indeed Milton is 'keeping English up', writing in a pure northern language and indulging in not a single Latin inversion or drawn-out sentence. How misguided, some might think, that he does so, not because he holds enlightened views on the language of small talk being the basis of all good poetry, but merely because he is accepting contemporary opinion on certain styles being appropriate to certain subjects. And when he comes to *Paradise Lost* he must needs once again bow to public opinion and write in a style remote from the virtuousness of his epitaph on Hobson.

Whether we like it or not, we are forced to admit that the heightened style of *Paradise Lost* was something demanded of him as an epic poet with a rigour against which there was no possible appeal. Now a very widespread notion of Milton's heightened style is that it was an arbitrary if not wantonly fabricated medium, the product of a man isolated from his age and hostile to it. Anyhow the whole onus of choosing it is commonly thrust on Milton. If some readers can realize that he chose it for the very opposite reason, in order to be at one with his age, they may look on it with initial favour rather than with their present repugnance. The epic convention to which Milton was bound resembles the inexorable need to satisfy a mixed audience which limited Shakespeare. What astonishes is the successful use to which both poets put their limiting conditions and the measure of freedom they both achieved within them.

My third consideration is the probability that far too much has been made of the supposed latinization of Milton's style. This latinization is quite a subordinate part of the necessary heightening just discussed, being mainly confined to short phrases and to the option of holding back the main verb in a way unusual in familiar English. Many of Milton's inversions do not go beyond the usual practice of most English poets. I grant a few of Milton's latinized phrases are irritating, even to a reader thoroughly familiar with his style: for instance Christ's opening words to Satan in *Paradise Regained*, after the wet night in the wilderness:

Mee worse than wet thou find'st not.

Others lose their queerness after a few readings and

often have the virtue of being short and concentrated.
Eve in book ten of *Paradise Lost* says to Adam:

> I will not hide
> What thoughts in my unquiet brest are ris'n,
> Tending to som relief of our extremes,
> Or end, though sharp and sad, yet tolerable,
> As in our evils, and of easier choice.

As in our evils, meaning *in such evils as ours* or *in view of
our evil plight*, may be a latinism (*ut in his malis*), but
obtrudes itself little. Many of the latinisms attributed
to Milton could be good English idiom just as well. In
this passage from Mammon's speech in the second
book of *Paradise Lost* where he advises the devils to

> seek
> Our own good from ourselves, and from our own
> *Live to ourselves*,

the last three words have been supposed to echo
Horace's

> ut *mihi vivam*
> Quod superest aevi.

But there is not the slightest need to insist on a latinization. Even if Milton coined the phrase to *live to
yourself*, it is a good English coinage and justifiable on
the analogy of *keeping to yourself*. Another mistake is to
see a latinization in every absolute participial clause
Milton wrote. When Shakespeare writes

> Good porter, turn the key,
> All cruels else subscribed,

it is not usual to insist that in the last phrase he was
deliberately imitating the Latin ablative absolute; nor
is the phrase 'one man gone, another takes his place'

usually considered latinized English; nor again do stockholders complain of ablative absolutes or distorted English when they receive dividends 'income tax deducted'. Why then insist that Milton is latinized when he uses such phrases? If you are intent on finding latinisms in Shakespeare, you will meet with wide success. Take, for instance, the line

As flies to wanton boys, are we to the gods.

How unnatural a perversion of the normal word-order of English speech: convincing proof that Shakespeare had been improving his small Latin at the time of *Lear*. Contrariwise, if you read Milton unobsessed with the notion that he could not write native English, you will find far less latinization than he is usually credited with. The mistake is due to Milton's past admirers quite as much as to his enemies, because in past years some misguided men thought it an absolute virtue to be 'influenced' by the classics, and it pleased Milton's admirers to find that influence even when it did not exist.

The main peculiarities or heightenings of Milton's style in *Paradise Lost* are quite unlatin, indeed quite alien to the genius of the Latin tongue. Mr Empson[1] has put his finger on the right spot when he talks of Milton's 'vague or apparently disordered grammar'. But the phrase needs quoting in its context.

People are now agreed in approving Milton's rhythms, and accepting his subdued puns without looking at them

[1] *Some Versions of Pastoral*, p. 161 (section on Bentley and Milton). He goes on to describe what beautiful effects this 'apparently disordered grammar' can yield.

closely. I don't know what is the normal view about his vague or apparently disordered grammar, which Bentley thought indefensible; especially the use of *and* or *or* when the sense needs more detailed logical structure. Pearce defended it very little. The chief reason for it is that Milton aims both at a compact and weighty style, which needs short clauses, and a sustained style with the weight of momentum, which requires long clauses.

In other words Milton wanted to have it both ways, to be both concentrated and ample; and to achieve this he packs his statements close but, that he may avoid any staccato effect, links them loosely by means of *and's* or *or's* (as Mr Empson says), or of vague appositions, or of participial constructions. By this same looseness of linkage Milton is entirely alien to the precise periodic structure of Latin oratory, or to the elegant logical neatness of a poet like Ovid.

But it is time to illustrate. And let me begin with an instance of Miltonic concentration:

> So passd they naked on, nor shund the sight
> Of God or Angel, for they thought no ill:
> So hand in hand they passd, the lovliest pair
> That ever since in loves imbraces met,
> *Adam* the goodliest man of men since born
> His Sons, the fairest of her Daughters Eve.

At first glance this is a simple and straightforward passage. (In passing, let it be asked, how can anyone, in view of passages of this kind, accuse Milton of writing perpetually in the Grand Style?) But in two places it is exceedingly compressed. Taken strictly, the phrase

> lovliest pair
> That ever since in loves embraces met

is nonsense. Adam and Eve could not meet, after they had ceased to live, in love's embraces; and that is the strict meaning of the passage. However, the reader is not worried and knows well enough, at a first reading, that by *lovliest pair that* Milton meant 'loveliest pair, lovelier than any who' and that before *met* one must supply *have*. The last two lines are also very compressed and similarly illogical. Adam could not be the goodliest of his own progeny, because he was not his own son, nor could Eve be the fairest of her own daughters, for the same reason. The full sense of the lines takes not a few words to express. 'Adam, goodliest of men, goodlier than all his male posterity, who were also his own children, Eve, fairest of women, fairer than all her female posterity, who were also her own children.' Not only are these lines compressed but they tempt one in their subtlety to use Mr Empson's critical method upon them, for we can get slightly different senses from

> *Adam* the goodliest man of men since born
> His Sons,

according to where we pause in the reading. I must not, however, dally with this temptation but make the more relevant points, first that all this compression and highhandedness with logic is not specifically Latin, secondly that these very qualities are not unrelated to the spoken tongue. True, Milton compresses with a rigour too daring for everyday traffic, yet the liberties he takes, the disregard of logic if the sense is plain, are those we insist on preserving in our ordinary speech. The passage I have quoted is not usually accused of lacking epic dignity. But within that dignity, what simplicity, what daring, and what freedom!

In writing thus I have ignored a good deal of earlier discussion on the logical lapses in this passage. Addison and Bentley both disapproved of them. Some of Milton's editors defended him by classical precedent, pointing out that if Homer could write ὠκυμορώτατος ἄλλων, and Horace write of a freedwoman *fortissima Tyndaridarum*, when she was very far from being one of the daughters of Tyndareus, Milton was at liberty to call Adam *the goodliest man of men since born his sons*. As a defence, such an observation is quite unnecessary and a piece of pedantry which compares ill with the common sense of Newton, who wrote, 'I believe a man would not be corrected for writing false English, who should say *the most learned of all others* instead of *more learned than all others.*' Nevertheless, Milton was probably aware of the classical precedent, when he wrote the passage, and wished his readers to give it a glance if they felt inclined. He wrote his lines to stand on their own feet as English, yet through a hint of Homer he was able to ensure the epic decorum demanded by his contemporaries: he was able to be English and international at one and the same time in accord with the dearest ideals of the Renaissance.

For a number of statements concentrated in themselves but loosely assembled into a single unit of sense, there is no better example than the exordium of book nine of *Paradise Lost.*[1] Lines 5–41 are but

---

[1] The whole passage is quoted below on pp. 165–166.

one sentence. Here the chief method of linkage is the apposition:

> Sad task, yet argument
> Not less but more Heroic,

and again with the typical Miltonic compression and vagueness of connection,

> Not sedulous by Nature to indite
> Warrs, hitherto the onely Argument
> Heroic deem'd, chief maistrie to dissect
> With long and tedious havoc fabl'd Knights
> In Battels feign'd,

where the appositional phrase *chief maistrie* cannot stand for less than, 'the chief skill in the describing of wars being...'. I am not certain that in this exordium Milton does not push this particular style of his too far, but what should be evident is that it is not in the least latinized except in an occasional detail like

> Mee of these
> Nor skilld nor studious, higher Argument
> Remaines.

The liberty to compress is common to the poets of all nations, while the loose structure linking weighty matter is a thoroughly English feature, comparable most nearly to the style of the more poetical prose-writers of the pre-Restoration period.

(Not only were these points of Milton's style alien to Latin, they were quite beyond the power of his imitators. Mr Murry's contention that you can write Miltonics but not Shakespeareans is entirely false. With Milton's high-handed and significant compressions and with his loose structure the eighteenth century had little sympathy; nor with all the sympathy in the world could it have got anywhere near them. Insisting on order and tidiness, it quite destroyed both the great simplicities and the great audacities of its original. Keats's first *Hyperion* may have Miltonic turns of phrase and may have been inspired by the general magnificence of *Paradise Lost*, but it lacks Milton's larger stylistic qualities, however superb it may be in its own right.)

In questioning the magnitude of Milton's stylistic debt to Latin, I did not mean to deny that Milton owed anything to the Latin poets. But to write your own language in a foreign way and to get help from a foreign poet are two quite different things. Virgil may have encouraged Milton to pack his sense, but that does not mean that Milton packed it in a Latin rather than an English manner. Similarly, when in the revised *Hyperion* Keats writes lines like these

Methought I stood where trees of every clime...
or
And when I clasp'd my hands I felt them not,
or
      a terror
That made my heart too small to hold its blood,

we may say that he was encouraged by Dante, without implying that his idiom is in any sense italianate.

Nor, once again, do I mean to deny that Milton in *Paradise Lost* exploited the Latin element in the English vocabulary. Walter Raleigh has pointed out how Milton used many Latin words in a double sense:

To the ordinary intelligence they convey one meaning; to a scholar's memory they suggest also another. It became the habit of Milton to make use of both values, to assess his words in both capacities. Any page of his work furnishes examples of his delicate care for the original meaning of Latin words.

What I should deny is that there is anything un-English in such a procedure, unless you are the sort of purist who believes it un-English to admit any sort of alien word (the sort of purist Keats appeared to have been on 21 September 1819). Latin loan-words were nearer to their source in Milton's day than in ours, and he had every right to exploit that still live propinquity. Milton manipulated the Latin element in our vocabulary in yet another way: he constantly set it close to the lowliest simplicity:

> The Sun that light imparts to all, receives
> From all his alimental recompence
> In humid exhalations, and at Even
> Sups with the Ocean.

This playing off the simple against the Latin element is central to the genius of the English language and as essential to Shakespeare and Thomas Browne as to Milton. Shakespeare's 'exsufflicate and blown surmises' or his 'multitudinous seas' stand for an ingrained native habit whose rightness is not questioned. Thomas Browne's most gorgeous latinity comes to rest in Germanic plainness:

And if, as we have elsewhere declared, any have been so happy, as personally to understand Christian annihilation, ecstasy, exolution, transformation, the kiss of the spouse, and ingression into the divine shadow, according to mystical theology, they have already had an handsome anticipation of heaven; the world is in a manner over, and the earth in ashes unto them.

Milton, in using the same process, was not letting English down but enriching one of its most precious inheritances.

The main point I wish to make in speaking of Milton's latinization is that if a good deal of it turns out to be English after all, the charge of remoteness or of writing English like a dead language loses much of its support.

I have made so far three pleas concerning the way the verse of Milton's later poems should be read. The first had to do with reassurance: a plea that the reader should recognize the unflagging potential presence of certain qualities which, though not thrust forward in the norm of Milton's verse, are hinted at from time to time. The second implored the reader to take into account contemporary critical notions of epic decorum. The third warned readers to beware of the notion, too glibly accepted by Milton's friends and enemies alike, that his style is seriously based on Latin or on any foreign tongue. A well-disposed reader could give the first and third of these pleas a trial, without any difficulty. The second plea is a far more serious matter. To have read oneself into the Miltonic decorum, to be able to take it for granted, are states attainable only after some labour. And that labour is as it were a fairly stiff entrance-fee, though certainly not stiffer than the parallel labour of mastering the conventions of Elizabethan drama. I cannot help suspecting that some of those who attack Milton's style have not read him closely enough to have assimilated the Miltonic decorum. Two of the most eminent, indeed, suggest so much by their own words. Mr Murry confesses that the back of his Milton still has something of the stubbornness it brought back from the binder. Mr Eliot says that you have to read Milton twice: once for the sense, and once for the sound. Might not further readings yield a more unified result?

Now, once we are familiar with the Miltonic decorum, there emerges a stylistic variety that was unsuspected before and with which Milton has never been sufficiently credited. If he had written more pieces in the styles of the lines on Hobson and on Shakespeare it would be far easier to demonstrate his stylistic range to those who can see no more in *Paradise Lost* than the superficial decorum. Yet within that decorum Milton passes freely from the most reverberant trumpet blasts to the most delicate cadences of speech. I will not illustrate the blasts: they, alas, have been taken far too widely as the universal rule in *Paradise Lost* and as the essential Miltonic norm. But I will quote a single passage showing the command that Milton had, within his decorum, of the rhythms of speech. It is Adam's answer to Eve, who in her extreme of penitence wishes to take all the blame of the Fall on herself:

> Unwarie, and too desirous, as before
> So now, of what thou knowst not, who desir'st
> The punishment all on thy self; alas,
> Beare thine own first, ill able to sustaine
> His full wrauth whose thou feelst as yet lest part,
> And my displeasure bearst so ill. If Prayers
> Could alter high Decrees, I to that place
> Would speed before thee, and be louder heard,

That on my head all might be visited,
Thy frailtie and infirmer Sex forgiv'n,
To me committed and by me expos'd.
But rise, let us no more contend, nor blame
Each other, blam'd enough elsewhere, but strive
In offices of Love, how we may light'n
Each others burden in our share of woe;
Since this days Death denounc't, if ought I see,
Will prove no sudden, but a slow-pac't evill,
A long days dying to augment our paine,
And to our Seed (O hapless Seed!) deriv'd.

Pre-eminent in this passage is the sinuous and varied movement of the verse following the flow and ebb of Adam's thought. The first few lines have the very accent of tender and broken speech: a prolonged pause after *unwarie*, a bigger unit thence down to *knowst not* containing the hushed parenthesis of *as before so now*, the prolonged third line with pauses on the strongly stressed *all* and *self*, and with a long pause after *alas*. Adam is caught up in pity of Eve's plight, in pure sentiment of outgoing sympathy. With no impulse to action, the rhythm falters brokenly. Then with *If Prayers* he imagines himself acting, going to the place of condemnation and asking pardon; and the rhythm mends itself into greater energy. But he knows that the imagining is fruitless and with *But rise* he relapses, not into the broken rhythms of unmitigated sympathy, but into an intermediate rhythm expressing sympathy joined with a plea for the restricted action within their powers. The last four lines, exquisitely sad and leisurely, put the case of Adam and Eve in a distant view and balance the close and pressing feelings of the opening. Outside Shakespeare and a few passages of the Elizabethan drama such perfectly modulated blank verse is not to be found in English.

I have no space to quote and discuss other instances of Milton's stylistic range:[1] let this one instance stand as a refutation of the charge of arterio-sclerosis.

In trying to refute the first of the two major charges commonly brought against Milton, that of forsaking common English speech and of hardening into a remote grandeur, I have perforce implied some defence of the second charge, that Milton's poetic method was inorganic. If, as I hold, Adam's speech to penitent Eve grew out of the situation and its needs, it must be unassailable. But this speech is not the only one in *Paradise Lost* and might be objected to as exceptional. And to strengthen my case for Milton's organic method I will discuss a passage which Mr Eliot chose as an example in the contrary sense.[2] It is the opening of the first speech Satan addressed to his subordinates after the command in heaven to do homage to the Son (*Paradise Lost*, v, 769):

> Thrones, Dominations, Princedomes, Vertues, Powers,
> If these magnific Titles yet remain
> Not meerly titular, since by Decree
> Another now hath to himself ingross't
> All Power, and us eclipst under the name
> Of King anointed, for whom all this haste
> Of midnight march, and hurried meeting here,
> This onely to consult how we may best
> With what may be devis'd of honours new

---

[1] For an admirable description of another great speech in *Paradise Lost* see Professor Stoll's article *Belial as an Example* in *Modern Language Notes*, 1933, pp. 419–427.

[2] *Essays and Studies of the English Association*, 1935, p. 35.

Receive him coming to receive from us
Knee-tribute yet unpaid, prostration vile,
Too much to one, but double how endur'd,
To one and to his image now proclaim'd?

Of this complicated speech Mr Eliot writes:

the complication of a Miltonic sentence is an active complication, a complication deliberately introduced into what was a previously simplified and abstract thought. The dark angel here is not *thinking* or conversing, but making a speech carefully prepared for him; and the arrangement is for the sake of musical value, not for significance.

To this I should say in passing that this stark antithesis between 'conversing' and 'making a speech carefully prepared for him' is a false simplification, because all dramatic writing of any value is a blend of the two. Polonius's advice to Laertes is a speech every bit as carefully prepared for him as the speech of Satan just quoted. But the main point is that Mr Eliot has missed the whole force of the speech's complication through ignoring the context. The situation is this. Satan refuses to do homage to the Son and has hurriedly collected his followers and taken them into his own dominions. In his palace

he assembl'd all his Train,
Pretending so commanded to consult
About the great reception of thir King,
Thither to come, and with calumnious Art
Of counterfeted truth thus held thir ears.

Satan's speech is *art*; the dramatic situation demands it: and he proceeds to say little in many high-sounding words with an art which even Mr Ramsay Macdonald might envy. The complication arises quite naturally out of the dramatic exigencies of the situation. Should anyone doubt it, he should go on and read the speech with which Abdiel interrupts Satan's cloudy rhetoric. It is clear, confident, and energetic, utterly opposed to Satan's in movement, and as closely dictated by the dramatic needs of the situation.

> O argument blasphemous, false and proud!
> Words which no eare ever to hear in Heav'n
> Expected, least of all from thee, ingrate
> In place thy self so high above thy Peeres.
> Canst thou with impious obloquie condemne
> The just Decree of God, pronounc't and sworn,
> That to his only Son by right endu'd
> With Regal Scepter, every Soule in Heav'n
> Shall bend the knee, and in that honour due
> Confess him rightful King?

I know well enough that by pointing out the dramatic relevance of these two speeches I have not proved that Milton was writing organically. Dramatic relevance can be faked with little trouble. It could be that Milton had carefully planned out the appropriately dramatic setting and sentiment in prose abstraction and then proceeded to translate his prose into the stereotyped poetic rhetoric of which he was a master. That Milton did not do this I cannot possibly prove, but, if he did and if this was his habitual poetic method, he ranks as an epic poet with Blackmore and Glover rather than with Camoens or Virgil. But Mr Welby and Mr Eliot and most of those who call Milton's style inorganic would not rate him so low. To them Milton is great by his art or by his music. But, if that art and music are great, they must corre-

spond to something in Milton's mind; they must be
the proper correlatives of it. If they are the unsatisfactory correlatives of what Milton professed as his
proper business, they must at least be the satisfactory
correlatives of something else—unless art drops from
the skies, a thing unattached to a human mind. And
if they are in some degree satisfactory correlatives, so
far will they be organic. The charge therefore that
Milton's style is simultaneously inorganic and magnificent reduces itself to the statement that Milton's poetic
strength is in the unconscious rather than the conscious
realm; and it would be far better if those who make
that charge did so in such terms. Having attempted
that topic elsewhere, I will not prolong it now.

Finally, let me point out with what extraordinary
difficulties Milton was beset in the matter of poetic
style through living just when he did. When Dr Leavis,
after an excellent analysis of a passage in *Comus*,[1] proceeds to pillory the style of *Paradise Lost* as exhibiting a
shocking decline in vitality and flexibility, he takes no
account of what the changing ideas of the age demanded. Being likewise so insistent that poets should
be 'aware of the contemporary situation', is he altogether just? If the changes Milton made in his style
correspond to the general trend, ought he to be
grudged the virtue of this 'awareness'? In any case
the change of style from Milton's early to his late verse
ought to be considered along with the changes that
were then taking place in the language of poetry.

In his most interesting book on *English Poetry and*

[1] *Revaluation*, pp. 47 ff.

the English Language Mr F. W. Bateson defines the changes that took place in the language of poetry during the lifetime of Milton. In the early part of the seventeenth century men used as many words as possible in as many ways as possible; and the connotative rather than the denotative side of language was developed. Words were pushed beyond their normal meanings, until 'the metaphysical writers by continually extending the common meaning of words gradually cut the ground away from under themselves'. A reaction was bound to follow, and it took the form of postulating a possible perfection or maturity of language. In other words, a denotative austerity superseded a love of connotative profusion. 'The Augustan achievement was by shearing words of their secondary and irrelevant associations to release the full energy of their primary meanings.' Now Milton suffered the extraordinary embarrassment of being thoroughly involved in both of the two conflicting currents, and he is the only seventeenth-century poet who attempted to combine both methods.

Mr C. S. Lewis's study of the readings in *Comus*[1] shows that Milton was sensitive to the change of feeling, even before the Commonwealth; he is ahead, reacting from profusion towards austerity. For instance the line

When the big wallowing flakes of pitchie clowds

is discarded altogether; while in a passage, itself omitted from the final version, *tough passado* becomes *tough encounter*. In *Paradise Lost*, as I have already

[1] *Review of English Studies*, April 1932.

mentioned, Milton is constantly striving to use simple words like *fair* and *joy* with the fullest charge of significance, thereby conforming to the Augustan ideal, while yet preserving his freedom to be startling and exuberant at times. I believe he took the only course suitable to a very great poet. To have clung to the antiquated method of profusion would have cut him off from the best sustenance he could get from his age; to have followed the new method without qualification would have cramped and injured him. Some kind of compromise was necessary, and it took all Milton's heroic force to effect it. We shall not quarrel with Peacock when he calls the two ages we are discussing the golden and the silver age of English poetry, though we need not follow him through the other metals. And he recognized Milton's intermediate position:

Milton may be said to stand alone between the ages of gold and silver, combining the excellencies of both; for with all the energy, and power, and freshness of the first, he united all the studied and elaborate magnificence of the second.

Moreover, though in places we may say, 'here Milton writes like an Augustan, there he prolongs the old Elizabethan exuberance of *Comus*', the general fusion is complete. When Satan says

> That Glory never shall his wrath or might
> Extort from me,

the words, none of them unusual, have the fullest denotative virtue that they are capable of, and yet they are charged with the dramatic sense and with a potential exuberance inherited from Elizabethan drama. Nevertheless, the fusion is so complete that in reading there is not the slightest sense of anything composite, and to force the above distinction is an effort if not an outrage. Mr Empson has an extremely interesting section[1] on one or two passages where he thinks Milton fell into absurdity. I fancy he exaggerates, but at least once I grant him his point. What is pertinent here is that he suggests that one particular effect, unsuccessful in Milton, would have come off in an Elizabethan. It is only natural that in his almost impossible position between two poetic epochs Milton should occasionally have come to grief: the wonder is that he came to grief so rarely.

[1] *Op. cit.* pp. 153 ff.

MILTON AND THE EPIC

(i) THE ENGLISH EPIC TRADITION

AFTER the great versions of the Bible, Pope's *Iliad* is the most serious translation in the English language. But it is serious for not quite the same reasons. Pope, indeed, revered his original with a feeling not far short of religious awe, but he revered something for him even greater than Homer: the abstract idea of the classical epic. For Pope, as for Milton and Dryden, the classical epic was no dead literary form, something brought to perfection by Homer and Virgil, and because perfected, therefore inimitable. No, it was a permanent ideal, which had indeed been worthily embodied by two authors of antiquity, which had perhaps been embodied by Tasso, but which could and should be embodied in the present age. There were, of course, in the neo-classic age other ideal forms, tragedy, comedy, and the idyll, for instance; but none of these could compare in seriousness with the epic. The Earl of Mulgrave in his *Essay on Poetry* (1682), a short handbook to Parnassus in the heroic couplet, leads up from lyric, through satiric and dramatic, to epic poetry, which has its home on the very top of the mountain.

> By painfull steps we are at last got up
> *Parnassus* hill, upon whose Airy top
> The *Epick* Poems so divinely show,
> And with just pride behold the rest below.

Heroick Poems have a just pretence
To be the chief effort of humane sence,
A work of such inestimable worth,
There are but two the world has yet brought forth,
Homer and *Virgil*: with what awfull sound
Each of those names the trembling Air does wound!
Just as a Changeling seems below the rest
Of men, or rather is a two legg'd beast,
So those Gigantick souls, amaz'd, we find
As much above the rest of humane kind.
Nature's whole strength united! endless fame,
And universal shouts attend their name!

Shakespeare, it is worth noting, though praised, has his home below the top of the mountain.

The Earl of Mulgrave is at one with the orthodox opinion of his age; and we should do well to remember, as the late Professor W. P. Ker liked to exhort us, that it was before a background of such extravagant homage to the epic form that Milton conceived *Paradise Lost*, Dryden toyed with an *Arthuriad*, and Pope translated the *Iliad* of Homer. In this lecture I shall inquire through what stages the epic passed to reach this Augustan eminence.

And now, the moment we leave the realm of the strictly classical epic, arises the difficulty of definition: what is to be included in the epic category? There are two ways of meeting the difficulty. The first is to include in the epic all works consciously included in it by contemporary opinion. Such are Spenser's *Faerie Queene*, Sidney's *Arcadia*, and Warner's *Albion's England*. The second is for me to give the definition I happen to fancy and to ask you to accept it temporarily for the purposes of this lecture. As I wish to include the first and second of the above works, but not the third, in the epic category, it will not serve my turn to accept contemporary opinion; and my only course is to give you my private notion of the epic.

The notion I prefer is extremely simple and flexible. Distinctions between authentic and artificial epics, attempts to confine epic to verse or to a special grand style, are hazardous and confusing. It is safer to require but three qualities of the epic: that it should be narrative on a large scale, that it should be so serious as to merit the epithet 'universal', and that it should be positive rather than critical. Some critics—and they have every right to do so if they wish—insist that this universality should arise from the characters. Without characters who worthily embody the universal elements in human nature, narrative remains on the hither side of the epic in the realm of romance. Thus Dr Mackail, in *Springs of Helicon*, notes the absence of real human beings in the *Faerie Queene* and calls that poem 'a romance wrapped in the imperial robes of the epic, but lacking her sceptre and crown'. But for my present purposes I prefer a looser definition, and would include in epic universality not only that of character, but that of a culture. For all its shadowy characterization the *Faerie Queene* embodied the Elizabethan culture, and it was acclaimed as such an embodiment. I could explain the third postulate—that epic should be positive rather than critical—by saying that, on a balance, epic in its narrative sphere should correspond to the tragic rather than to the comic in the dramatic sphere. Such a definition would include the *Iliad*, the *Divine Comedy*, the *Faerie Queene*, and *War and Peace*.

Aristotle thought tragedy superior to epic as a literary form, but the other critics of antiquity were not of his opinion. Homer was the greatest poet, and through him the epic form was exalted. That the greatest Latin poet should have had epic rather than dramatic inclinations confirmed this exaltation. Thus, in the Silver Latin age, the eminence of the epic form was such that poets attempted it, regardless whether it in the least corresponded to their own inner needs. In an earlier age Ovid had wisely shunned the straight epic and for his longest work chose a series of loosely connected tales (thus giving scope to his narrative power), while, to satisfy his rhetorical proclivities, he caused the tragic heroines of antiquity to churn up their souls in fantastic epistles to their absent lovers. But in the Silver Latin age the epic form was so powerful that an ambitious poet like Statius must needs use it for feelings of which it was not the most suitable vehicle.

For the hollowness of the Silver Latin epic there is a very good reason. Although the *Iliad* exhibits characters sufficiently universal to put that poem among the greatest epics, yet it sums up also a complete polity or culture. The *Aeneid*, too, is political: it attempts to render an imperial idea as well as a national rule of conduct. And it does so both through the story and through the hero. Thus the two great epics of classical antiquity are largely political. Now the later epic, though clinging to the traditional form, and in spite of Lucan, had no strong political faith with which to fill it. Hence its sterility. It did, however, prolong one quality which belonged to the epic from the first and which was strongly stressed by later critics, often to the detriment of other and perhaps more important qualities. I mean the notion implied in the synonym of the epic, the heroic poem. The author of the *Iliad* may have had little conscious notion that he was depicting a whole culture, or that in the changes that take place in the mind of Achilles he was rendering supremely well a regeneration pattern that may be the very core of tragedy. (I refer here to a theory put forward by Miss Maud Bodkin in her noteworthy book, *Archetypal Patterns in Poetry*.) But he certainly thought that he was commemorating the deeds of heroes. Whether in so doing he had any didactic intention is quite uncertain, but from Xenophon's time on, if not earlier, the *Iliad* was regarded as a store of heroic examples. Plutarch, in his essay *How a Young Man ought to hear Poems*, ignoring most of what we think important in Homer, looks on the great and good personages in his poems as models of conduct, much like the eminent Greeks and Romans whose lives he himself recounted. And Plutarch represented a large body of opinion. Anyhow, the notion of the pattern-hero was strong in the Silver Latin age, and it was destined to be the chief connecting link through the Middle Ages between late Latin and early Renaissance epic practice.

But there was another way of interpreting Homer and Virgil which both leads to a new type of epic and explains the barrenness of late Latin epic: the allegorical. Though this arose long before Christ, it did not take on its strongest significance till long after. It was applied with the greatest earnestness to Virgil and it reached a climax in the *Expositio Virgilianae Continentiae* of Fabius Fulgentius (sixth century A.D. ?), who interpreted the *Aeneid* as the progress of the human soul from birth (symbolized by the shipwreck in book one) to its triumph over the vices. Although this interpretation rivals in its improbability the remotest speculations of the wildest disciples of Freud, it is important enough in showing how the essence of the potential epic had changed, and why the late Latin epic was so ineffective. The late Latin poets had lost the political or social content that had been the life of the early epic without acquiring the true epic subject of the Christian era: the pilgrimage of the human soul on earth. If, then, Fulgentius was absurd as a critic, he was perfectly sound on the direction the epic ought to take in his own day.

It was not till the noon of the Middle Ages that Fulgentius's correct instincts were worthily fulfilled. For all its topical and political content the innermost significance of the *Divine Comedy* is the human pilgrimage from a mental hell to a mental Beatific Vision. And now we reach our first contact with the epic tradition in English. The medieval English poem which has the best epic pretension is *Piers Plowman*. Here, again, for all the accretions of political and social satire, and in spite of the very un-Dantesque issue of Do-best into a practical and not a visionary realm, there exists in the poem a residue, exiguous it may be, consisting of the great medieval subject, the progress and salvation of the soul of man.

Just as the classical epic, originally cultural as well as heroic in subject, lived on into an era when it was irrelevant, so, too, medieval interpretations and the characteristically medieval epic form lingered with fitful energy into the Renaissance. Golding, for instance, in his introduction to his translation of Ovid's *Metamorphoses*, allegorizes his author's meaning with a thoroughness not unworthy of Fulgentius. Stephen Hawes's *Pastime of Pleasure* is a would-be medieval epic, treating of the moral pilgrimage of man, but written when the vitality was leaving the tradition. Spenser, in the first book of the *Faerie Queene*, was great enough to revive the dying form and to give it perhaps its greatest poetic consummation in English; for the Red Cross Knight, though so much else, is the medieval Everyman who achieves through trial and suffering the pilgrim's ultimate goal. Among the humble the tradition lingered on for many years after Spenser and achieved another embodiment in Bunyan's *Pilgrim's Progress*. How, greatly modified and enriched, it reached yet one more embodiment about the same time, will be described near the end of this lecture.

For the origin of the characteristically Renaissance epic in England we have to go not to the spiritual strain exemplified in Langland, but to the heroic strain, which, though less serious in the Middle Ages than the spiritual, enjoyed a vast exploitation. One of the recognized functions of literature in the Middle

Ages was to commemorate the deeds of great men, whether Saints, authentically historical kings like Charlemagne and Richard I and Robert Bruce, or legendary figures like Hector or King Arthur. In this general desire to celebrate worthy men heroic poetry was merged in history, and history in all the improbabilities of romance. There were several reasons for commemorating great men: justice to their memory, historical truth, delight and edification of the reader. The first lines of Barbour's *Bruce* (which I quote in a modern translation)[1] will illustrate:

Stories are delightful to read, even if they be nought but fable. Therefore should stories that are true, if well told, have double pleasure for the hearer. The first pleasure is in the tale as a tale, and the second in the truth of it, that shows the happening right as it was. Thus truths wholesome for man's mind are made pleasant to his ear.

Fain would I, therefore, set my will, if my wit suffice, to put in writing a true tale, that it endure henceforth in memory, that no length of time destroy it, nor cause it to be wholly forgotten. For stories of old time, as men read, picture to them the deeds of the stout folk that lived of yore right as if done before their eyes. And surely praise is fairly due to those who in their time were wise and strong, who spent their lives in great labours, and often, in hard stress of battle, won right great prize of chivalry and acquitted themselves of cowardice. Such was King Robert of Scotland.

Observe that the edifying or didactic is but one of several reasons for the heroic story. Now the specifically Renaissance epic got a large part of its character by putting a heavy emphasis on didacticism and

[1] By George Eyre-Todd, Glasgow, 1907.

giving it a form which, though it grew out of the Middle Ages, became autonomous.

Signs of the change are to be seen, as one might expect, in some of the works of Petrarch and Boccaccio. There is in them a noticeable shift in the centre of seriousness, compared, say, with the seriousness of Dante. Dante minded most about the human soul and its salvation, even though he minded passionately about politics and culture. To him the poet was a philosopher first, however important as a teacher of political wisdom. For Petrarch and Boccaccio, theology and philosophy began to be less important than morality, and a morality fraught with great political significance. The change is, of course, closely connected with the beginnings of humanism, of a shifting of first values from the abstract to the actively human sphere. The inevitable result of this shifting was that heroic literature, dealing with the fortunes of great men, of secondary importance in the Middle Ages, had gradually to take the first place. For the medieval state of affairs consider two contemporary poems, *Piers Plowman* and Barbour's *Bruce*. The first, being in part concerned with abstract notions of holiness, is, for its age, the more serious work. By the age of Henry VIII the situation had been reversed.

As far as the English epic of the Renaissance is concerned, the result of this humanizing process is not to turn abruptly to the classical epic, but to seize on and modify a certain didactic element already present in the long medieval narrative. Roughly it can be said that here didacticism is mainly illustrative. The narrator tells his story for what it is worth, and then, if he likes, he illustrates a specific act by a general moral. When he was in his worst fortunes, Bruce's hostess on Arran prophesied a happy issue. Bruce was encouraged but did not altogether put faith in her words; whereupon Barbour inserts a pleasant little sermon upon the virtues and vices of prognostication. Similarly it was the business of the medieval, as of the classical, rhetorician to have a repertory of *exempla*, anecdotes, fables, etc., ready for the purpose of illustration or pointing a moral. Chaucer's Monk, when badgered by the Host for a diverting story, retaliates by attempting to bring out of his clerical cold storage his complete repertory of famous men, who, having fallen from prosperity, illustrate the vicissitudes of fortune. His tale is not really a tale at all, but an exasperating succession of unconnected *exempla*, as Chaucer shows he knew by making the Knight cut short the Monk in mid career. The change from medieval to Renaissance methods comes when what was but an illustration becomes the principal subject, when the hero is less a man who does things than one who, in doing them, embodies certain virtues and vices, in such a way that he serves as a great example, as a highly significant object-lesson, a figure of solemn and inspiring didacticism. Could the characters in the *Monk's Tale* cease to be mere illustrations and become serious embodiments of the caprices of fortune, then they would belong in spirit to the Renaissance. But the new didactic solemnity is to be seen not in Chaucer, but in Petrarch's *De Viris Illustribus* and

Boccaccio's *De Claris Mulieribus* and *De Casibus Virorum Illustrium*.

This notion of the great 'example' was to dominate much Renaissance literature. Its full importance was first recognized by Miss Lily Campbell in her book on Shakespeare's tragic heroes; but she confines it to the unfortunate and thus to tragedy, and omits to say how, in its beginnings, it was connected with contemporary politics. Petrarch, in the preface to his lives of illustrious men, said that he chose two sorts of theme, the one illustrating virtue, the other illustrating vice; the first showing what was to be followed, the second what to be avoided. Here, in embryo, is the Renaissance notion of epic and tragedy. Epic, it must be added, could include 'tragedy' within its compass, while tragedy was for long allowed to be in narrative as well as in dramatic form. Now the Renaissance 'example' differs from the medieval 'example' not only in elevating a mere illustration into the main subject-matter, but in being addressed to a definite class of person: the prince or at least some influential noble. Professor Huizinga, in *The Waning of the Middle Ages*, has vividly described how dependent in the fourteenth and fifteenth centuries, when the control of the Church was weakening, the countries of western Europe were on the personal character of their princely ruler. Again and again there were terrible object-lessons of how a weak or idle prince could ruin his country. For England the example of Henry VI is quite sufficient. Serious men were cruelly aware how vital it was to train the prince to be a good ruler; and the energies of serious literature were directed to that object. Its highest work was to educate the growing prince or to instruct the mature one. And its peculiar and most effective method was through the great example.

It is not the fashion to connect Lydgate with the Renaissance, yet he illustrates, in contradistinction to Chaucer, the characteristically Renaissance notion of the 'example'. His *Fall of Princes* is a versification of Boccaccio's *De Casibus Virorum Illustrium*, but he adds his own prologue, where he speaks at length of Boccaccio's warning to princes not to trust fortune but to take warning from those who had fallen. He praises Humphrey, Duke of Gloucester, Regent during Henry VI's absence in France. Humphrey is a scholar as well as a knight; he eschews idleness, hates heretics, and knows the lesson, taught by examples in Boccaccio's book, of avoiding confidence in fortune. Therefore, to give examples to princes in general, he has ordered Lydgate to translate Boccaccio's book. A second fifteenth-century exponent of this characteristically Renaissance notion is Caxton, whose prefaces contain some important critical material. In his prologue to the *Mirrour of the World* (1481), for instance, he says what he considers the objects of literature; and one of these is to provide nobles with reading that may keep them from idleness 'at such time as they have none other virtuous occupation'. It would be tedious to illustrate the 'example' notion profusely; it meets us throughout Renaissance criticism. But to show its vitality I give a quotation dating from the reign of James I. Thomas Heywood, the dramatist, wrote the following passage in his *Apology for Actors*:

In the first of the Olimpiads, amongst many other active exercises in which Hercules ever triumph'd as victor, there was in his nonage presented unto him by his tutor, in the fashion of a history acted by the choise of the nobility of Greece, the worthy and memorable acts of his father Jupiter: which being personated with lively and well spirited action, wrought such impression in his noble thoughts, that in mere emulation of his father's valour (not at the behest of his stepdame Juno), he perform'd his twelve labours.

Far from being a joke, this passage expounds a serious and orthodox theory of criticism and education.

To define the Renaissance epic as the history of a great man making good for the instruction of the ruling class of nobles would, of course, be too simple. There were other elements. First, learning was demanded of the epic. This demand was partly an inheritance of the medieval notion of the learned clerk, the sage who knew everything, partly the result of the way men regarded the newly discovered Homer. And they followed Plutarch in regarding him as a storehouse of learning and sententious morality. A second epic property had to do with patriotism. Through the new feeling for nationality arose the notion that you glorified your country by writing correct literature in your own language. Thirdly, an epic had to derive something from classical precedent, but it was not till the neo-classic period that this demand was at all exacting. As a general result the Renaissance epic became, like the classical epic, essentially cultural and political.

Now, although the theory of the Renaissance epic in England may have its first faint beginnings in the fifteenth century, much time elapsed before it animated any literature with epic pretensions. In the age of Wyatt and Surrey there was no poet great enough to attempt an epic task. Yet we may conjecture that if there had been he would have conformed to the 'example' theory and have drawn his inspiration from works like Elyot's *Image of Governaunce* or the *Golden Book of Marcus Aurelius*. In the interval between this age and that of Elizabeth the new learning established itself in Europe, Aristotle's *Poetics* were assimilated, and a set of rules was devised in Italy which was ultimately to be stereotyped into the neo-classic creed. According to these rules it was ordained, in spite of Aristotle's exaltation of tragedy and because of the prestige of Homer and Virgil, that the epic was the noblest of all literary forms. And it was inevitable that when the English Renaissance was at the full, the more ambitious among the academic poets should stake their reputations on the epic. Hence Sidney's *Arcadia* and Spenser's *Faerie Queene*, the two English productions next in time after *Piers Plowman* I should include in the epic category.

If you have accepted for the moment my definition of epic, you will be content to include the *Faerie Queene* within it. Not every one will be prepared to include *Arcadia*. For one thing, the description of the Arcadian landscape in the second chapter is better known than the book itself and has coloured men's conceptions.

There were hills which garnished their proud heights with stately trees: humble valleys whose base estate seemed comforted with refreshing of silver rivers: meadows enameled with all sorts of eye-pleasing flowers: thickets, which being lined with most pleasant shade, were witnessed so to by the cheerful disposition of many well-tuned birds: each pasture stored with sheep feeding with sober security, while the pretty lambs with bleating oratory craved the dams' comfort: here a shepherd's boy piping, as though he should never be old: there a young shepherdess knitting and withal singing, and it seemed that her voice comforted her hands to work, and her hands kept tune to her voice's music.

On the evidence of such a passage too many men (I will not say readers) have thought of *Arcadia* along with the *Faithful Shepherdess* rather than with the *Faerie Queene*. To do so is about as correct as to call *Paradise Lost* a pastoral fantasy on the sole evidence of the description of Paradise in Book Four. Actually, Sidney considered *Arcadia* an epic (of the Renaissance type, of course); his biographer speaks of its high didactic and political aim; and for years it was coupled with the *Faerie Queene* as the masterpiece of the Elizabethan age. Sidney's own testimony, oblique but unmistakable, is found in his *Defence of Poesy*. Early in this essay Sidney mentions the different kinds of poetry and puts the heroic at the head of the list. He then says that, although most poets use metre, it is not metre that makes the poetry:

Xenophon, who did imitate so excellently as to give us *effigiem iusti imperii*, the portraiture of a just empire, under the name of Cyrus (as Cicero saith of him) made therein an absolute heroical poem. So did Heliodorus in his sugared invention of that picture of love in Theagines and Chariclea. And yet both these writ in prose: which I speak to show, that it is not riming and versing that maketh a poet, no more than a long gown maketh an advocate; who though he pleaded in armour should be an advocate and no soldier. But it is that feigning notable images of virtues, vices, or what else, with that delightful teaching, which must be the right describing note to know a poet by.

I used to wonder, before I had read *Arcadia* properly, why Sidney troubled to be so emphatic about the heroic poem in prose, just as I had once wondered why, in the *Sacred Wood*, Mr T. S. Eliot had published an essay on the possibility of the poetic drama in our own day. And, just as Mr Eliot has recently supplied the answer by writing his two poetic dramas, *The Rock* and *Murder in the Cathedral* (not to speak of *Sweeney Agonistes*), so what Sidney had really in mind was his own epic ambitions. The reference to Heliodorus puts the matter out of doubt, for the revised *Arcadia* is, in structure, closely modelled on the *Aethiopica* of Heliodorus, of which Theagines and Chariclea are the hero and heroine. And in 'that feigning notable images of virtues, vices, or what else, with that delightful teaching', Sidney is simply repeating the 'example' notion which was the animating idea of the Renaissance epic. In sum, along with the doctrine, there is implicit Sidney's own ambition to write an orthodox didactic epic modelled on the *Aethiopica* of Heliodorus. Fulke Greville, who was Sidney's friend, in his *Life of the renowned Sir Philip Sidney*, mentions the 'example' notion in *Arcadia*, and particularly stresses its high political importance:

In all these creatures of his making, his intent and scope was, to turn the barren philosophy precepts into pregnant images of life; and in them, first on the monarch's part, lively to represent the growth, state, and declination of princes, change of government and laws, vicissitudes of sedition, faction, succession, confederacies, plantations, with all other errors or alterations in public affairs. Then again in the subjects' case: the state of favour, disfavour, prosperity, adversity, emulation, quarrel, undertaking, retiring, hospitality, travel, and all other moods of private fortunes or misfortunes. In which traverses, I know, his purpose was to limn out such exact pictures of every posture of the mind that any man, being forced in the strains of this life to pass through any straits or latitudes of good or ill fortune, might, as in a glass, see how to set a good countenance upon all the discountenances of adversity and a stay upon the exorbitant smiling of chance.

Fulke Greville is saying only what should be obvious to any reasonably careful reader of *Arcadia*; and it is a curious object-lesson in human carelessness that, from the end of the seventeenth century till a few years ago, *Arcadia* should have been taken as a not too serious pastoral instead of as a Renaissance epic into which one of the great Elizabethans poured all his stores of wit, wisdom, and ingenuity. It was reserved for an American, the late Professor Greenlaw,[1] to point once again to the true nature of *Arcadia*.

The *Faerie Queene*, though including the great

---

[1] In *Kittredge Anniversary Papers*, Boston, 1913.

medieval theme, is equally in accord with the Renaissance theory of the epic. If Pyrocles and Musidorus are patterns of princely chivalry, Euarchus of kingly wisdom, Pamela of Christian and stoical courage in misfortune, Cecropia of villainy, Spenser's characters are equally didactic, while in his letter to Raleigh, prefixed to his poem, he explicitly declares his Arthur to be the perfect pattern of epic hero. Spenser says that his aim—the typical educational aim of the Renaissance—is to 'fashion a gentleman'. And he does so through this perfect pattern:

I chose the history of King Arthur, as most fit for the excellency of his person, being made famous by many men's former works, and also furthest from the danger of envy and suspicion of present time. In which I have followed all the antique poets historical; first Homer, who in the persons of Agamemnon and Ulysses hath ensampled a good governor and a virtuous man...then Virgil, whose like intention was to do in the person of Aeneas; after him Ariosto...and lately Tasso....By ensample of which excellent poets, I labour to portrait, in Arthur, before he was king, the image of a brave knight, perfected in the twelve private moral virtues, as Aristotle hath devised.

Now in recent years there has been a distinct shift of opinion towards taking the *Faerie Queene* as something more than a pretty series of pageants and allowing it to speak for a whole civilization. With that shift I sympathize, and so sympathizing I should call the poem an epic. But what of *Arcadia*? Even if it attempts to be an epic, does it succeed? I answer that, for any one who has the leisure and the patience to read it slowly, it does. Like the *Faerie Queene* it is clogged with episodes inherited from the medieval romance, but, like the *Faerie Queene*, it gradually builds up an effect of high moral seriousness. The unfailing vitality of the prose rhythms matches the unfailing enchantment of Spenser's metre. And again, just like Spenser, at any moment and when least expected, the author may spring from the conventional into the thrilling. Out of many possible passages I quote, as an example of vital writing, the description the wicked Cecropia gives of herself in her pride to her son Amphialus:

I came into this country as apparent princess thereof and accordingly was courted and followed of all the ladies of this country. My port and pomp did well become a King of Argos' daughter; in my presence their tongues were turned into ears, and their ears were captives unto my tongue. Their eyes admired my majesty, and happy was he or she on whom I would suffer the beams thereof to fall. Did I go to church? It seemed the very Gods waited for me, their devotions not being solemnized till *I* was ready. Did I walk abroad to see any delight? Nay, my walking was the delight itself; for to it was the concourse, one thrusting upon another who might show himself most diligent and serviceable towards me. My sleeps were inquired after and my wakings never unsaluted, the very gate of my house full of principal persons who were glad if their presents had received a grateful acceptation. And in this felicity wert thou born, the very earth submitting itself unto thee to be trodden on as by his prince.

I do not wish to imply that *Arcadia* is as great literature as the *Faerie Queene*, but it is a work that has the same intentions and which springs from the same *ethos*. It should be thought of along with the *Faerie Queene*, a distinction not shared by any other Elizabethan production. In one respect it is much better than the *Faerie Queene*: that is, in respect of construction.

Heliodorus's *Aethiopica* is a late Greek romance with a wildly improbable and varied plot, but carefully constructed on the epic model with much of the story narrated by the characters retrospectively. Sidney, who follows Scaliger in classing Heliodorus with the great epic poets, maintains a very tight hold over a plot whose Heliodoran richness is swollen by material inherited from the medieval romance. To do so was an uncommon intellectual feat. It also betokens a conscientious classicism, alien to Spenser, and prophetic of the neo-classic age, a phenomenon matched by Sidney's being the first critic to introduce the newly invented dramatic unities into England.

There is a second fundamental element in which Sidney is more classical than Spenser: the motivation of the characters. As in his *Defence of Poesy* he shows an intelligent and intimate understanding of the *Poetics* of Aristotle (much of his argument being based on Aristotle's claim that poetry is more philosophical than history), so he applies to *Arcadia* the Aristotelian conception of the tragic hero. The main action of the story is precipitated by the ἁμαρτία of Basilius, a character more good than bad, who, instead of fulfilling his kingly duties, must needs worry about the future, consult oracles, and, to guard against the oracle's pronouncement, abandon his kingdom and immure his daughters. And there are other Aristotelian characters.

All the same, *Arcadia*, with its length, its bewildering variety of incidents, its fantasticness, its delight in pageantry, its political doctrines bearing the impress of Machiavelli, is an epic of the Renaissance rather than of the neo-classic variety. Although Camoens had already given the world a poem written in the vernacular, thoroughly expressive of contemporary thought, and yet cast in the strictest Virgilian form, England was still too wedded to the relics of medievalism to be able to use his example. And *Arcadia*, although showing the beginnings of classicism, served actually to encourage writers of narrative to prolong the tradition of the medieval romance into the seventeenth century.

A more truly transitional work, and the only Elizabethan narrative poem outside the *Faerie Queen* worth mentioning in the same breath with the epic, is Daniel's *Civil Wars*. Planned as an historical poem of twelve books, it was dropped after the eighth. Four books were published in 1595, when Shakespeare was in the middle of his Histories; and the date is significant because Daniel shared both the historical subject-matter and the political philosophy of Shakespeare. It is this philosophical earnestness that gives the poem its slight touch of an epic quality. In execution it is plain and economical, the very antithesis of *Arcadia*, and looks forward to the age of good sense. Daniel frequently imitates Virgil in detail, but such imitation goes beyond detail, betokening a true and conscious allegiance to the chastened form of the *Aeneid*. Daniel's is the first English narrative poem with something genuinely neo-classic about it.

In the first half of the seventeenth century the nature of the English would-be epic poetry is fantastically mixed. There are the most antiquated survivals of the Middle Ages, Arcadianisms with a metaphysical flavour and a developed neo-classical movement all co-existing. Of the first, Thomas Heywood's *Troia Britannica* and *The Exemplary Lives and Memorable Acts of nine the most worthy Women of the World* are examples. *Troia Britannica* purports to deal with world-history. It begins with the Creation in Hebrew and Greek mythology, is voluble on Greek and Trojan legend, and huddles up a summary of English history into the last section. The other work is constructed quite frankly on the medieval model of the Nine Worthies. Chamberlayne's *Pharonnida* imitates the heroics and the variety of *Arcadia* but dissolves them into structural chaos and makes them unreadable by the most frigid monotony of metaphysical wit. Such gorgeousness as adorns this recently over-praised poem is due more to the accidental conjunctions of a wantonly and riotously opulent vocabulary than to any genuine control. The first decidedly neo-classic poem is Cowley's *Davideis*.

Although the *Davideis* is a better poem than is usually allowed, only in one particular does it make any *vital* contribution to the English epic. That contribution is metrical. By using the heroic couplet and at times using it well, Cowley promotes an epic process which culminated in Pope's *Iliad*.[1] Apart from this vital contribution the *Davideis* has plenty of historical interest. It shows the pressure of academic theory

[1] Cowley was not the first English poet to use the couplet for verse with epic pretensions. His chief forerunner was Sylvester in his translation of Du Bartas. It is the way Cowley uses the couplet that matters.

concerning the epic for the first time in English literature finding complete issue in action. (This time was
about 1638, for, according to Sprat's *Life and Writings
of Cowley*, most of the *Davideis* was finished while
Cowley was 'a young student in Cambridge'.)

It is usual to father the academic theory of the strict
classical epic on the Italian critics of the Renaissance.
Actually, it had never quite died since the Silver Latin
age. Dr Mackail, in his *Latin Literature*, has remarked
how much resemblance there is between the latest
Latin and the earlier Renaissance epic written in
Latin. And between Claudian and Petrarch's *Africa*
there was some continuity. The notion persisted that
Virgil was the greatest poet and that the Latin hexameter, the *heroicum carmen*, was the noblest metre. And
there is a succession of heroic poems in Latin hexameters (or elegiacs) more or less closely connected
with the pagan tradition. There are, for instance,
Fortunatus's *Life of St Martin* and Bede's *Life of St
Cuthbert*, both in hexameters and both influenced by
Virgil. An anonymous Italian wrote a poem on the
Emperor Berengarius (crowned in 915), celebrating
him as if he were a hero of antiquity and taking verses
from Virgil, Juvenal, and Statius. Joseph of Exeter
wrote an *Antiocheis* (now lost) describing the heroic
deeds of Richard I. It must have had some relation
to the classical epic. In the same century Walter of
Châtillon wrote an *Alexandreis*[1] telling the story
of Alexander from youth to death. It contains

[1] See F. J. E. Raby, *A History of Secular Latin Poetry in the Middle
Ages*, Oxford, 1934, ii, 73.

the correct epic features, including a description of Darius's shield. But it follows the ordinary, unepisodic, and un-Virgilian time-sequence. It is useless to pretend that this tradition had the vitality of the vernacular allegory; but there it was. And its function was to encourage Petrarch in his *Africa* and Vida in his *Christiad* to resuscitate the classical epic in all its rigidity and with all its trappings, to perpetuate a form which, though never truly vital in the Renaissance, at last came into its own in the neo-classic age, and was perfected in *Paradise Lost*. During the Renaissance proper we must picture an ever growing belief in the pre-eminence of Homer and Virgil, continually reinforcing the notions that the epic was the supreme form and that excellence in poetry could be reached only by the severest imitation of classical models. For years this academic theory would affect practice not at all, or but partially. Then at last a man gives it full heed and puts it into action; and the neo-classic age has begun.

I mention the variety of heroic verse in the first half of the seventeenth century because I wish to suggest it as the background of Milton, who, for all his alleged aloofness, was in truth extremely sensitive to contemporary practice and critical opinion. Milton wrote his preface to *Samson Agonistes* because he wished to placate Puritan opinion on stage-plays and to prove to the academic reader that he was following the rules of Aristotle. I fancy he wrote his hot disclaimer of rhyme in the note prefixed to *Paradise Lost* to justify himself against the metrical precedent of the *Davideis* and the rise of the heroic couplet, of which he could not have been ignorant. Milton's own critical dicta are in close accord with Davenant's preface to *Gondibert*. Realizing this situation we may be better disposed to agree that Milton deals, either by acceptance or rejection, with the whole of the previous epic tradition in England.

The Renaissance epic was predominantly cultural and political, as against the medieval epic, which was religious and concerned itself with personal salvation. Milton's *Arthuriad*, had it been written, would have been of this Renaissance kind, though embodied in the strict neo-classic form with episodes and formal epic similes and diversified with the riches of Milton's mind. But events so fell out that the *Arthuriad* was never written and that Milton grew to think differently about politics. When he comes to write his great poem, politics have become less important than the fate of the individual soul. The result is that he turns against the whole heroic tradition of the Renaissance, and with a vehemence that betrays how strong a hold that tradition must have had on his allegiance. So at least the opening of his culminating book, the ninth, seems to say:

> No more of talk where God or Angel Guest
> With Man, as with his Friend, familiar us'd
> To sit indulgent, and with him partake
> Rural repast, permitting him the while
> Venial discourse unblam'd: I now must change
> Those Notes to Tragic; foul distrust, and breach
> Disloyal on the part of Man, revolt,
> And disobedience: On the part of Heav'n
> Now alienated, distance and distaste,

Anger and just rebuke, and judgment giv'n,
That brought into this World a world of woe,
Sinne and her shadow Death, and Miserie
Deaths Harbinger: Sad task, yet argument
Not less but more Heroic than the wrauth
Of stern *Achilles* on his Foe pursu'd
Thrice Fugitive about *Troy* Wall; or rage
Of *Turnus* for *Lavinia* disespous'd,
Or *Neptun's* ire or *Juno's*, that so long
Perplex'd the *Greek* and *Cytherea's* Son;
If answerable style I can obtaine
Of my Celestial Patroness, who deignes
Her nightly visitation unimplor'd,
And dictates to me slumbring, or inspires
Easie my unpremeditated Verse:
Since first this Subject for Heroic Song
Pleas'd me long choosing, and beginning late
Not sedulous by Nature to indite
Warrs, hitherto the onely Argument
Heroic deem'd, chief maistrie to dissect
With long and tedious havoc fabl'd Knights
In Battels feign'd; the better fortitude
Of Patience and Heroic Martyrdom
Unsung; or to describe Races and Games,
Or tilting Furniture, emblazon'd Shields,
Impreses quaint, Caparisons and Steeds;
Bases and tinsel Trappings, gorgious Knights
At Joust and Torneament; then marshal'd Feast
Serv'd up in Hall with Sewers, and Seneshals;
The skill of Artifice or Office mean,
Not that which justly gives Heroic name
To Person or to Poem. Mee of these
Nor skilled nor studious, higher Argument
Remaines, sufficient of itself to raise
That name, unless an age too late, or cold
Climat, or Years damp my intended wing
Deprest, and much they may, if all be mine,
Not Hers, who brings it nightly to my Ear.

The glory of *Paradise Lost* is that it resumes the essential medieval theme and combines it with Renaissance culture and exuberance and with neo-classic compression of form. *Paradise Lost* is a mental pilgrimage: the loss of one paradise and the finding, on this earth, of 'a Paradise within thee, happier farr'. That this paradise should have affinities with Stoicism and the Renaissance rather than with Dante does not prevent the poem's concerning the essentially medieval subject of the soul's pilgrimage. In still another way the theme of Milton's poem is medieval. Heywood's *Troia Britannica* shows that the old medieval subject of universal history (exemplified in *Cursor Mundi*) was not dead in the seventeenth century. *Paradise Lost*, for all its compression, deals with universal history from the creation of the angels to the final doom.

After Milton, the miraculous synthesis of medieval, Renaissance, and modern dissolves, and the emphasis falls, as before, on culture. Dryden's epic, had it been written, would have embodied the neo-classic faith in civilization as against fanaticism and in royalism as against mob-rule. It is ironical that in the age when the epic idea was strongest, when the pre-eminence of Homer was not to be contested, the angels were particularly afraid of treading and the fools particularly prone to rush in. Dryden shirked the original epic, while Sir Richard Blackmore came forward with three or four.

I began with Pope's *Iliad* and I end with it. Not that I can begin to comment on the qualities of that splendid work. As a translation of Homer, it is far closer to the essential qualities of the original than is generally allowed. But in addition, it is one of the supreme English products of the epic impulse and Pope's masterpiece. Through its rhythms, its frequently balanced sentences, its civilized tone, it speaks for its age, while its fervour and the intense seriousness that pervades it spring from the finest qualities of Pope's personality. If you take exception to these statements, remember the enthusiasm with which the age greeted it; remember that Pope spent the best years of his life working at it, mostly in the country, in a spirit of cloistral fervour and that Samuel Johnson, who did not praise excessively, called it 'that poetical wonder, a performance which no age or nation can pretend to equal'.

(ii) THE GROWTH OF MILTON'S EPIC PLANS

TILL recent years Milton was habitually regarded as a proud, isolated man, who planned his poems according to his own ideas of classical precedent without deigning to heed what his English colleagues thought or did. His evolution as an epic poet was private and simple. From early years he meant to be a great poet. He educated himself to that end. As his period of education drew to a close, he planned an epic on Arthur. This plan he discarded in favour of a tragedy, the subject of which after various castings round, was to be that of the Fall of Man. He got so far with it as to write a few lines of the prologue. Then, politics got the better of poetry for a spell; and when, in middle age, Milton was able to complete his life-work, he returned to the epic, retained the subject of his projected play, and wrote *Paradise Lost*.

The notion of isolation has been responsible for putting Milton on an eminence, good or bad, that has made him different from other poets. It certainly colours Mr Belloc's recent book; for it was Milton's isolation, his personal arbitrary daring in making decisions, combined with his overwhelming poetic power, which for Mr Belloc made it possible for him to give the last fatal blow to the Catholic tradition in England. And when Mr Eliot makes Milton responsible for breaking up the Elizabethan synthesis of thought and feeling and for damaging the English language, he may be arguing on similar premises.

But the movement the other way, the movement both to resurrect the social Milton of his first biographers and to set him as a poet firmly in his own age, has grown so strong that it is bound before many years to oust the traditional notion, which still, it must be granted, generally prevails. And the gain for Milton will be great. He will be spared a kind of idolatry that cannot but be punctuated with suppressed laughter; and his unique poetic gifts, instead of suffering the embarrassment of being pedestalled and smitten with a very dubious brand of limelight, will show up healthy but not the less striking in a normal seventeenth-century setting. Take, for instance, the battle in heaven from the sixth book of *Paradise Lost*. Readers have bowed to its sublimity, yet the profane have tended to groan at Satan's puns and the whole notion of introducing cannon into heaven. Professor Grierson has reminded us that nothing is more normal to the fantasy of the age than such a notion. No reminder could be more salutary. Reading the sixth book we should be able to accept the cannon as we accept the peculiarities of any age and to be impressed by the culminating emergence of the Son, without any suppressed sense that the whole episode inclines towards the ridiculous.

As to the narrower question of Milton's evolution as an epic poet, I shall now try to show how little isolated Milton was from contemporary theory and practice.

Milton (according to what remains of his writings) first broke silence concerning his poetic ambitions in July 1628, when at the age of nineteen he delivered the annual Vacation Exercise for the entertainment of the Cambridge undergraduates. That he should have thus used this public occasion argues something very different from the instinct of isolation; and the actual lines show him acutely sensitive to contemporary poetry. He begins by attacking (even while partly practising) a contemporary mode of extravagance. He deprecates

> those new fangled toys, and triming slight
> Which takes our late fantasticks with delight,

and he goes on to set forth the kind of poetry he is ambitious of writing. He aspires after some graver subject,

> Such where the deep transported mind may soare
> Above the wheeling poles, and at Heav'ns dore

Look in, and see each blissful Deitie
How he before the thunderous throne doth lie,
Listening to what unshorn *Apollo* sings
To th' touch of golden wires, while *Hebe* brings
Immortal Nectar to her kingly Sire:
Then passing through the Spherse of watchful fire,
And mistie Regions of wide air next under,
And hills of Snow and lofts of piled Thunder,
May tell at length how green-ey'd *Neptune* raves,
In Heav'ns defiance mustering all his waves;
Then sing of secret things that came to pass
When Beldam Nature in her cradle was;
And last of Kings and Queens and *Hero's* old,
Such as the wise *Demodocus* once told
In solemn Songs at King *Alcinous* feast.

Milton is in the habit of meaning what he says, and we shall not do this passage any evidential violence if we scrutinize it closely. He enumerates three types of poetry he would like to turn his chief talents to. The first concerns the gods and Apollo's hymns in heaven, and refers, I believe, to some kind of exalted lyric; in fact to a poetical kind which, many years later,[1] he still thought of practising, 'those magnific odes and hymns, wherein Pindarus and Callimachus are in most things worthy'. Callimachus's first hymn, to Zeus, would indeed be a perfectly appropriate song for Apollo to sing on Olympus. The second type, dealing with natural philosophy and the creation of the world, suggests Hesiod's *Theogony*, the first book of the *Metamorphoses*, and more particularly the *First Week* of Du Bartas. The last type is the straightforward heroic, for Demodocus sung the dispute

---

[1] In *Reason of Church Government*, Bohn, ii, 479.

between Achilles and Odysseus over strategy after the death of Hector, and the actual capture of Troy.

Now it is remarkable that at the early age of nineteen Milton should already have been weighing in his mind two kinds of 'epic' (according to contemporary notions) so different from each other as Du Bartas's scientifically inquisitive account of the Creation and the classical heroic. And the inference is that Milton as revealed for the first time was normally sensitive to his age. He was no isolated neo-classic, bent on nothing but a Virgilian rigidity, but open to those multifarious notions that make the Renaissance epic so protean a literary kind. The type of epic the Renaissance *per se* stood for was indeed the heroic, the kind that exhibited a hero who by doing great deeds was a pattern of behaviour to the contemporary prince or gentleman. But the Middle Ages died hard, and more than one medieval narrative form prolonged a hardy vitality into the seventeenth century. Du Bartas's poem on the Creation and on a part of subsequent Jewish mythology unites, as Mr George Coffin Taylor[1] points out, the medieval strain of biblical narrative (exemplified in *Cursor Mundi*) with the encyclopaedic content of the medieval 'Mirror' literature. Sylvester published his translation in 1605, which, as the successive editions showed, continued popular well past the date of Milton's *Vacation Exercise*. True to contemporary taste, Milton allows his ambitions to project themselves less into the remoter academic strictness of Vida's *Christiad* or Tasso's

[1] In *Milton's Use of Du Bartas*, Cambridge, Mass., 1934, pp. 9–12.

Jerusalem Delivered than into the immensely popular scientific and Protestant didacticism of Sylvester's huge translation.

But there is yet another connection in Milton's poem with the contemporary epic. One of the characters (*Relation*) in the masque of Scholastic terms to which his lines refer was named Rivers, and Milton uses his name for a digression on the rivers of England:

> Rivers arise; whether thou be the Son,
> Of utmost *Tweed*, or *Oose*, or gulphie *Dun*,
> Or *Trent*, who like some earth-born Giant spreads
> His thirty Armes along the indented Meads,
> Or sullen *Mole* that runneth underneath,
> Or *Severn* swift, guilty of Maidens death,
> Or Rockie *Avon*, or of Sedgie *Lee*,
> Or Coaly *Tine*, or antient hallowed *Dee*,
> Or *Humber* loud that keeps the *Scythians* Name,
> Or *Medway* smooth, or Royal Towred *Thame*.

As poetry these lines are the most masterly in the whole poem, being free from the slight sense of strain that pervades those already quoted. And they are entirely Miltonic, uttering a music that issues from the very core of Milton's being and yet fastidiously precise, full, and appropriate in thought. Further they suggest big tracts of poetry then popular and they look forward to more than one of Milton's later ventures. These smooth-running couplets, dealing with English geography, derive immediately from Browne's *Britannia's Pastorals*,[1] whose first two parts were published in 1613 and 1616, the second part therefore but twelve years

---

[1] It is certain that Milton knew this poem well at some period of his life, as a copy exists with his annotations.

before Milton's poem. But the references to early British mythology suggest that Milton, like Browne's seniors Spenser and Drayton, connected a geographical scene with a complete framework of Tudor patriotism. The cumulative force of the references is undoubted. The maiden of whose death the Severn was guilty is Sabrina, daughter of Locrine, himself son of Brutus, founder of the British nation; while the previous reference to the earth-born giant suggests the inhabitants found by Brutus and Corineus in Albion. The Dee is 'hallowed' because frequented by the Druids. Humber received its 'Scythian' name from the invader in the times of Brutus's sons. Finally the Thames is called royal-towered not only to recall Windsor and Hampton but also, probably, to connect the royal houses of Tudor and Stuart with the early British Kings.

The full story, but recently recovered, of how British myth and its Tudor connections affected Elizabethan literature is one of the quaintest and most fascinating in literary history. As far as I know, the chief credit of recovering it belongs to the late Professor Edwin Greenlaw of Johns Hopkins University. Most of it can be found in this author's *Studies in Spenser's Historical Allegory*.[1] But his discoveries have been amplified by several other authors. In particular I must mention Miss Roberta F. Brinkley's *Arthurian Legend in the Seventeenth Century*,[2] a book enthralling in its content though to my thinking not correct in all its conclusions about Milton's proposed *Arthuriad*.

[1] Baltimore, 1932.   [2] Baltimore, 1932.

To put the matter with all possible brevity, Henry Tudor, of illustrious Welsh descent, when he landed in Wales before the battle of Bosworth, was acclaimed by some of his countrymen as the fulfiller of the old prophecy of Merlin that Arthur would return, having never died, and reunite Britain. Coming to the throne as Henry VII he fostered the myth by causing the heralds to trace his ancestry back to the British Kings, and by naming his eldest son Arthur. Nor did the other Tudors let the matter drop. The return of Arthur was in the legends to bring with it an age of gold. 'It was the prophecy of the return of the golden age with Arthur that Elizabeth turned successfully to her own use to win the confidence of the people in her claims to the throne after the period of war and confusion following the death of Henry VIII.'[1] It would have been quite against the course of nature for the poets to have missed using this topical turn given to an already extant mythological material. Spenser used it to the full. Professor Greenlaw has shown that Arthur's pursuit of the Fairy Queen symbolizes (among other things of course) the notion that only in Elizabeth could the reincarnation of Arthur find its full issue. Warner in *Albion's England* and Drayton in *Polyolbion* also exploit British myth and Tudor pretensions.

Drayton's *Polyolbion* suggests a further type of poetry and brings us back to Milton's lines. However varied a form the Renaissance epic may have taken, it was usually patriotic in intention. Mr Lewis F. Ball has

[1] Brinkley, p. 3.

shown that the geographical poem with a patriotic intent goes back to early Tudor times.[1] Spenser, who strove to include every possible variety within his vast epic, perpetuates the type in his procession of the rivers which came to celebrate the marriage of the Thames and Medway.[2] But it was Drayton who made geography the basis of his English epic, *Polyolbion*, grafting on to his main theme the whole history of his country from Troy till modern times, including of course the British legends from Brutus to Arthur and Cadwallader. Mr Ball has proved that *Polyolbion* ranked as an epic, Drummond in particular considering the poem as the only epic England had to be proud of. Now *Polyolbion's* publication was not completed till 1622, only six years before Milton's *Vacation Exercise*. Milton can hardly have escaped reading it, and it must have been fresh to him. Though the metre of his description of the rivers is Browne's, and though Spenser furnished him with a quite sufficient model, yet the union of geography with British myth and with the touch of royalism was so specifically Drayton's, that Milton probably had him too in mind. Be that as it may, by hinting at the geographical poem yet excluding it from the passage where he talks seriously of his epic ambitions, Milton tells us that he is aware of this literary kind but does not take it seriously as epic.

To sum up so far, Milton's *Vacation Exercise* shows him vividly aware of contemporary English poetry:

[1] *The Background of the Minor English Renaissance Epics* in *English Literary History*, i, 63–89.
[2] *Faerie Queene*, iv, ii.

of the 'fantastics' of his age, of Sylvester's Du Bartas, of the heroic poem, of Browne the pastoral romancer, of Drayton ambitious of epic fame through geography and myth. And he indicates his own opinions and preferences.

The next reference to Milton's literary ambitions comes a year and a half later. Writing to Diodati in Latin elegiacs (*Elegia Sexta*) in the Christmas season of 1629, and immediately after his own coming of age, Milton speaks simultaneously of his own spare living and of the epic poet's need to live sparely. Wine may help Anacreon and Horace, but Homer had to be Pythagorean in his diet. And all his specific references to the heroic poem are to the *Odyssey*, as if he were now dreaming of writing his epic on this model rather than on that of Du Bartas. A few months later he wrote the fragment on the Passion, and there is here too the suggestion that he had the strict classical epic in his mind, though not a classical subject. He says that Christ is his theme, but though committed to lyric at the moment, he must needs mention Christ as an epic hero, while, partly to make it clear that he has not forgotten classical precedent, he hints that Christ is another Heracles. So much it is legitimate to infer[1] from his address to Christ as

Most perfect *Heroe*, try'd in heaviest plight
Of labours huge and hard, too hard for human wight.

In the fourth stanza Milton speaks of his own lyric

[1] Professor Merritt Y. Hughes in his note to this passage sees the reference to Heracles too. For his development of the Christ-Heracles analogy see his introduction to *Paradise Regained*, sections 3 and 4.

intentions in dealing with the Passion, but betrays his present interest in the epic by recalling how others have treated the life of Christ more largely:

> These latter scenes confine my roving vers,
> To this Horizon is my *Phoebus* bound;
> His Godlike acts, and his temptations fierce,
> And former sufferings other where are found;
> Loud o're the rest *Cremona's* Trump doth sound;
>   Me softer airs befit, and softer strings
> Of Lute, or Viol still, more apt for mournful things.

Cremona's Trump refers to Bishop Vida, native of Cremona, and to his *Christiad*, that fine product of the high Renaissance, in which he narrates in Virgilian hexameters and with the strictest machinery of the classical epic the history of Christ. It is quite possible that at the time of his sixth elegy Milton not only dedicated himself to epic poetry but contemplated the history of Christ as the subject of his future epic. The *Nativity Ode* and the *Passion* would be studies for it; and when Milton leaves the second poem unfinished with a note that the subject was 'above the years he had', he may have said farewell not to the *Passion* alone but to the above phase of epic ambition.

Professor J. H. Hanford[1] has shown that Milton's account of his own poetical interests in the *Apology for Smectymnuus* can be accurately applied to his extant works up to the time of his return from Italy. Milton there tells us that after his youthful absorption in the Latin elegiac poets and in the sonnets of Dante and Petrarch and a solemn self-dedication to heroic poetry,

[1] In the *Youth of Milton* and more shortly in the appendix to *A Milton Handbook*.

'I betook me among those lofty fables and romances, which recount in solemn cantos the deeds of knighthood founded by our victorious kings, and from hence had in renown over all Christendom.' Milton's own Latin elegies with their abundant Ovidian imitations illustrate the first phase, his early sonnets, including the Italian, the second. The neophytic and ascetic tone of *Elegia Sexta* fits well enough with his self-dedication to heroic poetry. So it may be conjectured that he began to be seriously taken up with the writers of romance after *Elegia Sexta* and the two poems I have associated with it, that is towards the end of his University career and in the Horton period. Anyhow in *L'Allegro* and *Il Penseroso*, when he mentions narrative poetry, his old favourite the *Odyssey* and the *Christiad* have dropped out; he is silent about any classical epic and speaks of the romancers alone. The 'throngs of Knights and Barons bold' and the rest in *L'Allegro* suggest Boiardo and Ariosto (Milton's Commonplace Book proves he knew Boiardo). In *Il Penseroso* his romance reading is probably English. Chaucer's *Squire's Tale* is definitely referred to, while the lines that follow the reference point to Spenser:

> And if ought els, great *Bards* beside,
> In sage and solemn tunes have sung,
> Of Turneys and of Trophies hung;
> Of Forests, and inchantments drear,
> Where more is meant then meets the ear.

At this point the reader may easily object that Milton knew Spenser from an early age and that a reference to him in *Il Penseroso* has no significance. To which I reply that my experience is that the more Milton's poems are studied, the more apt one finds them to reflect his interests and studies at the time. There is in truth more danger of paying too little heed to his hints than of reading into them too much. For myself I am pretty confident that with *Il Penseroso* begins a long period when Milton sees himself the third in succession to Chaucer and Spenser and when his epic ambitions centre in romantic matter. Both Du Bartas and the *Odyssey*, the chosen models for imitation in the *Vacation Exercise*, recede, and from now till the time of the Civil War Milton's thoughts turn to 'the deeds of knighthood founded by our victorious kings, and from hence had in renown over all Christendom': to Arthur, Charlemagne, or Godfrey. And the period culminates in the attempt at an *Arthuriad*.

Nor was there anything archaistic in those thoughts in the years 1631 to 1639. For one thing, the British legend and Tudor patriotism which Spenser exploited in the *Faerie Queene* had not ceased with the Stuarts. On the contrary James I was hailed alternatively as second Arthur or second Brutus, not only because of his Tudor descent but because his ancestor Fleance, son of Banquo, married the daughter of Griffith Llewelin, last of the native Welsh Kings.[1] Charles I on his accession was similarly honoured. In 1633 Carew's *Coelum Britannicum* and in 1636 Davenant's *Britannia Triumphans* (both masques) contained much British material. In 1634 Malory's *Morte d'Arthur*

[1] Brinkley, *op. cit.* p. 16. And I make free use of this book in the rest of this paragraph.

was republished (for the first and last time in the century). Thus Milton was entirely in harmony with contemporary practice when in *Comus* (1634) he introduces the legend of Sabrina, as found in Geoffrey of Monmouth, Spenser, and Drayton. All the same Milton cannot by this time have been ignorant of a serious drawback of this romantic material. Not long after Milton's birth, when James I began offending many Englishmen by claiming his Divine Right as King, the more democratic scholars sought in Saxon law and custom a counterpoise to the royal claims. It was this political motive that initiated the beginnings of Anglo-Saxon research in the early seventeenth century and which tended to degrade the authority of Geoffrey of Monmouth, chief sponsor of early British myth, which had indeed been questioned from the time of Polydore Virgil onwards. There arose the growing tendency for British myth to be associated with the King and his supporters, and for Anglo-Saxon history to be associated with Parliament and its rights. Arthur, however, was discredited more gradually than the other British Kings. Stories of him could be held even by the more scientifically minded to be part fact and part fiction. As Bacon said of Arthur in his *History of Henry VII*, 'there is truth enough to make him famous, besides that which is fabulous'. Milton then was quite sufficiently in the fashion if he gave attention to Spenserian material, but he risked running counter to the political party he favoured.

It is worth noting that even just before the time when

Milton most earnestly contemplated an *Arthuriad*, there is a reference to the epic which is closer to the *Vacation Exercise* than to *Il Penseroso* or *Mansus*. In the Latin poem to his father, which I date 1637, after mentioning the hieratic function of poetry and the songs of heaven, Milton mentions just one kind of earthly poem, the heroic:

> Tum de more sedens festa ad convivia vates
> Aesculea intonsos redimitus ab arbore crines,
> Heroumque actus, imitandaque gesta canebat,
> Et chaos, et positi late fundamina mundi,
> Reptantesque Deos, et alentes numina glandes,
> Et nondum Aetnaeo quaesitum fulmen ab antro.[1]

The acts of heroes and their function as 'examples' fit in perfectly with Renaissance theory and Spenserian practice and a possible *Arthuriad*. But chaos and the

[1] *Ad Patrem*, 44–49. I am indebted to Professor A. B. Cook for an explanation of the penultimate line, which no annotator or translator has hitherto shown he understands. *Reptantes Deos* suggest initially snake-gods like Asclepius or monsters like Briareus, but these do not accommodate themselves to a diet of acorns. Professor Cook points out that *reptare* can refer to an infant crawling and that Milton is speaking of the infancy of the gods. In that primitive, pre-agricultural age, acorns and other nuts were the common food. He paraphrases the line, 'when the gods were mere crawlers, and the powers that be were nurtured on acorn-mash'.

To this (and to the other quotations from Milton's Latin poems) I add Cowper's translation:

> Then sat the bard a customary guest
> To share the banquet, and, his length of locks
> With beechen honours bound, proposed in verse
> The characters of heroes and their deeds
> To imitation; sang of Chaos old,
> Of Nature's birth, of gods that crept in search
> Of acorns fallen, and of the thunder-bolt
> Not yet produced from Aetna's fiery cave.

creation show that Milton continued to be haunted by the theme of Hesiod and Du Bartas.

Nor could the recollection of Du Bartas have been the only inducement away from strict Renaissance doctrine to the Middle Ages. Milton, it is acknowledged, was deeply read in Spenser. Now, however orthodox Spenser professed to be in his preface to the *Faerie Queene* and however conscientiously he strove to imitate the ancients in practice, it yet remains true that his poem is far more medieval than the *Orlando*, not to speak of *Jerusalem Delivered*. He may outdo Virgil in the thoroughness in which he plunges *in medias res*, yet he perpetuates the one medieval theme that in seriousness outgoes all others.

You can never give any one meaning to any part of the *Faerie Queene*, but the preponderating theme of the first book, of far greater weight than the patriotic identification of the Red Cross Knight with St George, is the pilgrimage of the soul. The Knight is more than Holiness; he is Everyman. Endowed with the native virtue of the ordinary decent man, he prospers for a little, overthrowing the grosser forms of error. But he cannot survive the pressure of the world, the flesh, and the Devil from his own resources. His abode in the House of Pride weakens him, and through weakness though not active vice he is captured by Orgoglio. Prince Arthur, who rescues him, can stand for different ideas in different parts of the poem, or for more than one at the same time. As the knight's rescuer he stands beyond doubt for heavenly Grace.[1] I can cite

[1] See *Faerie Queene*, I, viii, 1 and 19.

Professor Grierson in support, who calls Arthur in this context, 'the Protestant conception of that prevenient grace of God without which no human virtue can achieve anything'.[1] After his rescue the Red Cross Knight is put through a course of penance and religious instruction, is led by Faith, Hope and Charity to the realm of contemplation, where he has a vision of the New Jerusalem. Fortified and regenerate he descends to kill the dragon. In sum the first book of the *Faerie Queene* is a Divine Comedy in minature.

The adventures of Guyon in book two are cast in somewhat the same mould; but a fuller opulence has entered it, the colours are more gorgeous, and the tone is more ethical and less religious. The Middle Ages are less obvious.

With the third and fourth books comes a great change. Mr C. S. Lewis[2] has written so well on Spenser that I dislike differing from him in any way. But when he makes a general claim for an overwhelming dominance of Ariosto over the form of the whole poem, I cannot entirely agree. There may be plenty of indebtedness of detail to Ariosto throughout; but it is not till books three and four that Spenser is truly Ariostan. But here he makes a quite fresh start and gives us poetry imitating the mazy plot and the clear-cut characterization of Ariosto. With what success, is here irrelevant. I omit the fifth and sixth books of the *Faerie Queene* as they add nothing to my present purpose.

[1] *Cross Currents in English Literature of the Seventeenth Century*, p. 51.
[2] *The Allegory of Love*, chap. vii.

Now Milton was so alien in temperament from Ariosto that he was unlikely to be much affected by the specifically Ariostan qualities in Spenser and anyhow he could draw direct on Ariosto; but I cannot see how he could have escaped being profoundly influenced all through his life by Spenser's version of the medieval theme of the soul's pilgrimage. It must have been permanently present in his mind, even in periods like the one under consideration when his poetic plans were being laid on other lines; and when we find it emerging in *Paradise Lost* and *Paradise Regained* we need feel no surprise, but recognize its emergence as the fulfilment of something long ago existing and demanding scope.

As to Milton's immediate plans for a heroic poem, now in process of formation, he must have found in Spenser anything but a definite lead. Spenser's shadowy Arthur could never do for the pattern of his hero, with Aeneas or Rinaldo to choose from. Nor could Spenser's clumsy reachings after classical form have satisfied the stricter neo-classic theories now growing powerful among the more academic in Milton's day. We must believe that Milton read Spenser more for his matter than for his style. Spenser's religious sense, his revival of the old British myths (which Milton clearly adored), and his patriotism must all have lain very near his heart. How he intended to use the Spenserian matter will be conjectured later.

I do not know if anyone has connected *Lycidas* with Milton's epic plans, but I fancy that this poem along with the almost contemporary letter to Diodati (23 September 1637) anticipates the clear references to an *Arthuriad* contained in *Mansus* a year later. In the letter Milton writes

What am I thinking about? you ask. So help me God, of immortality. What am I doing? Growing wings and learning to fly; but my Pegasus can only rise on tender pinions as yet, so let my new wisdom be humble.

Standing alone, this passage need not mean anything at all definite. Coming before *Lycidas* and *Mansus*, it refers, I believe, to a specific *Arthuriad*. That the old British legends were running in Milton's head is shown by two passages in *Lycidas*, while the second of them suggests his treating them very seriously indeed. First, Milton locates the haunts of the nymphs who might have protected Lycidas in Denbighshire, Anglesea, and by the Dee. Appropriately enough, since King sailed from Chester; yet, had not druidical lore been actively present in Milton's mind, he need not have used it. No one would have marked its absence. The second passage is

The fable of *Bellerus* old,
Where the great vision of the guarded Mount
Looks toward *Namancos* and *Bayona's* hold.

That Milton first wrote *Corineus* for *Bellerus* makes this passage the richer in mythological content. Corineus was Brutus's companion in the original settlement of Britain. He was an efficient giant-killer and received Cornwall for his pains. But Milton had a geographical meaning to convey, and Land's End, which he had reason to describe, was known as Bellerium. So he substituted Bellerus for Corineus, suggesting, I take it, that as Misenum was so called in Virgil after Misenus buried there, Bellerium took its name from the tomb of a local giant. It was an anonymous 'literary friend' of the Rev. Henry J. Todd who first identified Namancos T. (T. = *tierra*) in the map of Galicia in Mercator's Atlas of the editions between 1613 and 1636. It is marked there as the district of the extreme north-west of Spain, her Land's End. Bayona, farther south, is marked as an important fortress. Several Elizabethan authors mention the unimpeded sea-view between Land's End and Finisterre. We owe a great debt to Mr Todd's literary friend. He has made more precise and more effective one of Milton's most successful imaginings: his picture of the great Archangel on the mount named after him looking across the sea to Spain. That picture has been spoken of in an earlier section and needs no comment here. But the connection of British myth with Spain and with embattled Spain is another matter. British myth was connected with Tudor patriotism. Tudor patriotism rose to its height at the defeat of the Spanish Armada. Picturing the guardian archangel's protective gaze towards the Spanish stronghold we should be wrong not to let our minds glance at that event. And we should probably be wrong if we did not infer that at the time Milton wrote *Lycidas* British myth culminating in the rout of Spain was the chosen subject of his epic.

Such a definite pronouncement about *Lycidas* would be rash but for the tone and the contents of

Mansus. Written during Milton's Italian journey, *Mansus* is above all a patriotic poem and it strengthens the hints of patriotism in *Lycidas* I have sought above to draw out. Moreover, besides containing the well-known explicit statement of the projected *Arthuriad*, it continues the druidical and other mythological references introduced into the earlier poem. Milton salutes Manso as the patron of Tasso, strives at great length to establish a poetic vindication of his own country, and enlarges on his own poetical plans, closing with the wish that he might be as lucky as Tasso in acquiring a patron. The gist of his defence of English poetry is that there have been English poets, especially Chaucer and Spenser (already hinted at in *Il Penseroso*) and that in Druid times the British lays were not unknown in Greece. It is worth quoting the lines concerning the latter theme, to compare with *Lycidas*:

> Nos etiam colimus Phoebum, nos munera Phoebo
> Flaventes spicas, et lutea mala canistris,
> Halantemque crocum (perhibet nisi vana vetustas)
> Misimus, et lectas Druidum de gente choreas.
> (Gens Druides antiqua sacris operata deorum
> Heroum laudes imitandaque gesta canebant)
> Hinc quoties festo cingunt altaria cantu
> Delo in herbosa Graiae de more puellae
> Carminibus laetis memorant Corineida Loxo,
> Fatidicamque Upin, cum flavicoma Hecaërge
> Nuda Caledonio variatas pectora fuco.[1]

[1] Lines 38-48:
> We too serve Phoebus; Phoebus has received
> (If legends old may claim to be believed)
> No sordid gifts from us, the golden ear,
> The burnished apple, ruddiest of the year,

Here Milton, taking from Callimachus the names of the nymphs, Loxo, Upis, and Hecaërge, daughter of the North Wind, creates the elegant fiction that they were early Britons. Loxo was the daughter of Corineus, sent with her comrades from the band of druidical singers to a Delian festival, and still remembered in Delian tradition. The Druids and their poetry, Corineus: these were the early British elements in the first version of *Lycidas*.

Not only is the poem patriotic: it is animated with an intense admiration for Italy. Milton was almost obsessed with the notion that the cold Hyperborean climate of England might damp his intended wing; and the very emphasis with which he urges that it *can* produce poets argues a sense of inferiority. It is not unreasonable to suppose that Milton would at this time have liked to model his epic on some Italian pattern.

Milton's pronouncement in *Mansus* about his *Arthuriad* had better be taken along with his similar one in *Epitaphium Damonis*. They are complementary: taken together and considered in the light of what has

> The fragrant crocus, and, to grace his fane,
> Fair damsels chosen from the Druid train;
> Druids, our native bards in ancient time,
> Who gods and heroes praised in hallowed rhyme.
> Hence, often as the maids of Greece surround
> Apollo's shrine with hymns of festive sound,
> They name the virgins, who arrived of yore,
> With British offerings, on the Delian shore;
> Loxo, from giant Corineus sprung,
> Upis, on whose fair lips the future hung,
> And Hecaërge, with the golden hair,
> All decked with Pictish hues, and all with bosoms bare.

been said already, they tell us pretty plainly the kind
of poem Milton had projected. In *Mansus* he wishes
fate would give him a patron like Manso,

> Si quando indigenas revocabo in carmina reges,
> Arturumque etiam sub terris bella moventem;
> Aut dicam invictae sociali foedere mensae,
> Magnanimos Heroas, et (O modo spiritus adsit)
> Frangam Saxonicas Britonum sub Marte phalanges.[1]

Here the suggestion is that the main theme will be
Arthur defeating the Saxons; but to whom does
indigenas reges refer? Certainly to the British kings of
legend other than Arthur. But if only to them, what
point in referring to the prophecy of Merlin that
Arthur was still alive below ground? I can only think
that Milton meant to reiterate the legend that Arthur
was re-embodied in the house of Tudor. These are the
relevant lines from *Epitaphium Damonis*:

> Ipse ego Dardanias Rutupina per aequora puppes
> Dicam, et Pandrasidos regnum vetus Inogeniae,
> Brennumque Arviragumque duces, priscumque Belinum,
> Et tandem Armoricos Britonum sub lege colonos;
> Tum gravidam Arturo fatali fraude Jogernen
> Mendaces vultus, assumptaque Gorlois arma,
> Merlini dolus.[2]

[1] Lines 80–84:

> Should I recall hereafter into rhyme
> The Kings and heroes of my native clime,
> Arthur the chief, who even now prepares,
> In subterraneous being, future wars,
> With all his martial knights, to be restored
> Each to his seat around the federal board;
> And oh, if spirit fail me not, disperse
> Our Saxon plunderers, in triumphant verse.

[2] Lines 162–168:

> Of Brutus, Dardan chief, my song shall be,
> How with his barks he ploughed the British sea,

The references here are many and out of their time order. There is the landing of Brutus with his wife Imogen, daughter of Pandrasus, at Richborough to found the British Kingdom; Brennus and Belinus, sons of Dunwallo, six hundred years later; Arviragus from the time of the first Roman landing; the colonization of Armorica at the time of the Saxon invasions; and finally the birth of Arthur and the wiles of Merlin. Nothing specific here about Arthur's future; but it was Merlin to whom the prophecies about it were attributed.

Taking *Lycidas*, *Mansus*, and *Epitaphium Damonis* together, I conclude that Milton's long-projected *Arthuriad* was to be a patriotic poem of vast range, beginning with the Trojans in Britain, dealing with British history up to the defeat of the Spanish Armada, and having Arthur as the hero. We need not be surprised at the bulk, seeing that when Milton did come to write an epic, the time scheme began with the creation of the angels and ended with Doomsday. Further, such vastness had been included in the *Faerie Queene* and could be paralleled in Warner's *Albion's England* and Thomas Heywood's *Troia Britannica*. Can we conjecture into what form the poem

> First from Rutupia's towering headland seen,
> And of his consort's reign, fair Imogen;
> Of Brennus and Belinus, brothers bold,
> And of Arviragus, and how of old
> Our hardy sires the Armorican controlled,
> And of the wife of Gorloïs, who, surprised
> By Uther, in her husband's form disguised
> (Such was the force of Merlin's art) became
> Pregnant with Arthur of heroic fame.

would have been cast? I think we can, in the light of what Milton said in *Reason of Church Government*. It is not always possible to know, when he airs his poetical ambitions in this pamphlet, how far he refers to the past and how far to a conjectural future.[1] But he certainly refers back a great deal. Now when he speaks of the epic form, he names only one recent writer of epic, Tasso; and he names him twice. There was every reason why Milton should have looked to Tasso for guidance. He must have heard his praises from Manso's lips. He must have recognized him as the poet who reduced the exuberant form of Ariosto to neo-classic proportions. Moreover, in *Jerusalem Delivered* there was just that mixture of history and magic that was inherent in the story of Arthur in the England of 1639. As Tasso had Ariosto as his predecessor, so Milton had Spenser, whose form was predominantly Ariostan. I conclude that Milton meant to use Spenser as Tasso had used Ariosto. He would adopt the total historical and patriotic material of Spenser and recast it in the neo-classic form of Tasso. One difference there was bound to be. Milton obviously could not feel towards Charles I as Spenser felt towards Elizabeth. His Arthur reincarnate could be no king. He must be the genius of the English people instead, of which notion a famous passage in

[1] Mr William R. Parker (*Modern Philology*, xxxiii, 49–53) gives reasons for robbing the passage of all specific reference and reducing it to a defence, for the benefit of his pious readers, of three literary forms. It may well have been such in part, but that Milton should not have been closer to his own plans than Mr Parker allows seems to me, in view of other literary passages, extremely unlikely.

Areopágitica gives the general sense though it might almost be a specific reminiscence as well:

Methinks I see in my mind a noble and puissant nation rousing herself like a strong man after sleep, and shaking her invincible locks.

As to the writing of the epic, Milton tells us in *Epitaphium Damonis*[1] that he had tried to make a start a few days before—very soon, that is, after his return to England—but that he found the task too great for the poetic instrument at present at his command. Does this mean that he at once dropped the notion of an *Arthuriad* altogether? It is hard to say, but to do so would have been in accord with certain trends of contemporary opinion.

That Milton continued for several years to contemplate a patriotic epic is certain; but that Arthur would have remained its subject is doubtful. Miss Brinkley[2] has shown that the legend of Arthur reincarnate had the fate of becoming associated with party politics. It became a Royalist affair. On the other hand the Parliament men set up the Anglo-Saxons against the early British, whom they derided as unhistorical. Once the Civil War began and Milton had entered party politics, it would have been very difficult for him to retain as his hero the idol of his opponents.

Whether or not the Civil War expelled Arthur from the epic, it is certain that it influenced Milton's plan in one way. Believing that some great blessing of God was in the act of being granted his country, Milton

[1] Lines 155–159.   [2] *Op. cit.*

would have no need to go back to the Armada for his final issue; he could fittingly end in the present day. And in the leaders of the Parliament he can find the embodiment of the heroic virtues he means to celebrate. He therefore elects himself the panegyrist of the revolution. In his first pamphlet, written some year and a half after *Epitaphium Damonis*, he makes this pronouncement about himself:

Then, amidst the hymns and hallelujahs of saints, some one may perhaps be heard offering at high strains in new and lofty measures to sing and celebrate thy divine mercies and marvellous judgments in this land throughout all ages; whereby this great and warlike nation, instructed and inured to the fervent and continual practice of truth and righteousness, and casting far from her the rags of her old vices, may press on hard to that high and happy emulation to be found the soberest, wisest, and most Christian people at that day, when thou, the eternal and shortly expected King, shalt open the clouds to judge the several Kingdoms of the world, and distributing national honours and rewards to religious and just commonwealths, shalt put an end to all earthly tyrannies, proclaiming thy universal and mild monarchy through heaven and earth.[1]

In this land throughout all ages: Milton's patriotic poem is still to cover a great field of English history.

In *Animadversions upon the Remonstrant's Defence*, written a few months later, Milton is less confident, God's work has not yet been accomplished. 'Oh perfect and accomplish thy glorious acts!' he prays, and then (but only then)

he that now for haste snatches up a plain ungarnished present as a thank-offering to thee which could not be

[1] Bohn, ii, 418.

deferred in regard of thy so many late deliverances wrought for us one upon another, may then perhaps take up a harp and sing thee an elaborate song to generations.[1]

Then perhaps: this vagueness is remote from the present enthusiasms of *Mansus* and *Epitaphium Damonis*.

What was now passing in Milton's mind can be guessed from the dramatic themes noted in the Trinity Manuscript, roughly contemporary with the *Animadversions*. The entries in the Manuscript consist of a few detailed, serious plans for a play and of lists of subjects jotted down casually from Milton's reading. There are many points of interest in both types of entry. First, we see that, though Milton never dropped the notion of an epic and still favoured a patriotic heroic subject, he was at this moment more concerned with a play. Second, the detailed plans for *Paradise Lost*, the favourite subject among those seriously expounded, show in the list of characters decided affinities with the medieval drama. Personifications like Conscience, Justice, Mercy, Faith appear in all the drafts. It looks as if Milton's hankering after the greater abstraction of medieval forms had been active underground all the time he was meditating the heroic poem and, when the urgency of the latter form slackened, had at once taken the opportunity to make itself felt. Next, the sources from which all the plots are taken are either the Bible or early English and Scottish history. Finally, there is a queer entry. Among the many notes of subjects for plays occurs a single suggestion for an epic:

A heroical poem may be founded somewhere in Alfred's

[1] *Ib.* iii, 72.

reign, especially at his issuing out of Edelingsey on the Danes; whose actions are well like those of Ulysses.

A passage from Milton's *History of Britain* gives his proposed subject in some detail.

Meanwhile the king about Easter, not despairing of his affairs, built a fortress at a place called Athelney [=Edelingsey] in Somersetshire, therein valiantly defending himself and his followers, frequently sallying forth. The seventh week after he rode out to a place called Ecbrytstone in the east part of Selwood: thither resorted to him with much gratulation the Somerset and Wiltshire men, with many out of Hampshire, some of whom a little before had fled their country; with these marching to Ethandune, now Edindon in Wiltshire, he gave battle to the whole Danish power and put them to flight. Malmsbury writes that in this time of his recess, to go a spy into the Danish camp, he took upon him with one servant the habit of a fiddler; by this means, gaining access to the king's table and sometimes to his bed-chamber, got knowledge of their secrets, their careless encamping, and thereby this opportunity of assailing them on a sudden. The Danes, by this misfortune broken, gave him more hostages, and renewed their oaths to depart out of the kingdom. Their king Gytro or Gothrun offered willingly to receive baptism and accordingly came with thirty of his friends to a place called Aldra or Aulre near to Athelney and were baptised at Wedmore; where Alfred received him out of the font and named him Athelstan. After which they abode with him twelve days and were dismissed with rich presents. Whereupon the Danes removed next year to Cirencester, thence peaceably to the East-Angles, which Alfred, as some write, had bestowed on Gothrun to hold of him; the bounds whereof may be read among the laws of Alfred.[1]

Here is proof that even if Milton still contemplated an *Arthuriad*, Arthur was not the only possible heroic

[1] Bohn, v, 320–321.

subject. But I fancy we can go further. One interesting feature of the proposed themes in the Manuscript is that they are all, in the view of Milton and his contemporaries, *true*: coming from Holy Writ or well-attested history. Legend, other than scriptural, has disappeared. I think it probable that Milton, now definitely under the influence of Parliamentary thought, has abandoned the legendary and Royalist Arthur for the historical and constitutional Alfred, and that more generally he has yielded to that demand for scientific truth, whose growth in the century Mr Willey has described with such learning and charm.[1] It is interesting, too, that Milton should compare Alfred to Ulysses, recalling his early Odyssean ambitions in the *Vacation Exercise* and his account of epic poetry in *Elegia Sexta*. It is possible not only that he has now turned from Arthur as a subject but that he is beginning to dislike the whole romantic matter of the Renaissance epic and to seek a stricter imitation of the classics.

The great autobiographical passage in *Reason of Church Government* confirms the hesitancy visible in the two previous prose pamphlets and in the Trinity Manuscript. I mean hesitancy as to an immediate policy. General policy is clear enough. The epic comes first and it is to be national. Milton has been considering

what king or knight, before the conquest, might be chosen in whom to lay the pattern of a Christian hero. And as

[1] B. Willey, *The Seventeenth Century Background*, 1934. For Milton and his choice of a 'true' epic subject see pp. 219 ff.

Tasso gave to a prince of Italy his choice whether he would command him to write of Godfrey's expedition against the infidels, or Belisarius against the Goths, or Charlemain against the Lombards...it would haply be no rashness, from an equal diligence and inclination, to present the like offer in our own ancient stories.

That Milton's epic is still to be patriotic and contemporary is clear from the *Apology for Smectymnuus*. Here, speaking of the ruling majority of the Long Parliament, he hopes he may some day commemorate their deeds more worthily.

With this last pamphlet, written about March 1642, direct evidence for Milton's epic plans ceases till the beginnings of *Paradise Lost*. We leave Milton resolved on a patriotic poem; we find him actually writing something totally different. How did he come to change?

Miss Brinkley sees in the Roundhead hostility to British myth the reason why Milton dropped Arthur and assumed the Fall as his subject. It may be a sufficient reason for dropping Arthur, but not for dropping the orthodox heroic poem. For Milton had considered Alfred, who was peculiarly appropriate as a hero at the time of the Commonwealth. I agree with Mr Willey that the trend of the time was strongly towards a sacred subject, for among mythologies only that of the Bible retained the kind of credence likely to support a poet in a scientific age. But there are plenty of heroic stories in the Bible; and if Milton had truly wanted to write a heroic poem he could have used the theme of Samson without difficulty. Some more fundamental reason is necessary. I see no need to change the opinions expressed in my *Milton*: namely that Milton could not write an epic in praise of his country after he believed that his country had failed in its crisis. When he came to believe this is pretty clear. *Areopagitica* is transitional. It contains some of the patriotic enthusiasm that would have gone to his historical epic; but it also looks forward in dogma to *Paradise Lost*. Soon after, beginning with his sonnet, 'I did but prompt the age', Milton grows disillusioned with his country. The *History of Britain* contains passages bitterly censuring the Parliamentary Government between the First and Second Civil Wars and coldly criticizing the national character:

For Britain, to speak a truth not often spoken, as it is a land fruitful enough of men stout and courageous in war, so it is naturally not over-fertile of men able to govern justly and prudently in peace, trusting only to their mother-wit; who consider not justly, that civility, prudence, love of the public good more than of money and vain honour, are to this soil in a manner outlandish.... Valiant indeed and prosperous to win a field; but to know the end and reason of winning unjudicious and unwise; in good and bad success alike unteachable. For the sun, which we want, ripens wits as well as fruits; and as wine and oil are imported to us from abroad, so must ripe understanding and many civil virtues be imported into our minds from foreign writings and examples of best ages: we shall else miscarry still and come short in the attempts of any great enterprise.[1]

How, feeling thus, could Milton possibly write a patriotic epic, 'recall the British kings and crush the Saxon bands beneath the valour of the Britons'?

[1] Bohn, v, 240.

Milton was for years after to *act* the patriot, but the sentiments of the passage quoted are moving towards his last words on the subject. Writing to Peter Heimbach in 1666 he said:

For the virtue you call statesmanship (but which I would rather have you call loyalty to my country), after captivating me with her fair-sounding name, has, so to speak, almost left me without a country.... One's country is wherever it is well with one.

What confirms my opinion that the passage quoted from the *History of Britain* explains why Milton abandoned the heroic poem is that it resembles in tone the opening lines of *Paradise Lost*, book nine, where Milton explicitly repudiates the traditional martial theme of the epic. Oblivious of the bellicose pronouncements of his earlier years, he now calls himself

Not sedulous by Nature to indite
Warrs, hitherto the onely Argument
Heroic deem'd, chief maistrie to dissect
With long and tedious havoc fabl'd Knights
In Battels feign'd; the better fortitude
Of Patience and Heroic Martyrdom
Unsung; or to describe Races and Games,
Or tilting Furniture, emblazon'd Shields,
Impreses quaint, Caparisons and Steeds;
Bases and tinsel Trappings, gorgious knights
At Joust and Torneament; then marshal'd Feast
Serv'd up in Hall with Sewers, and Seneshals;
The skill of Artifice or Office mean,
Nor that which justly gives Heroic name
To Person or to Poem. Mee of these
Nor skilld nor studious, higher Argument
Remaines, sufficient of it self to raise
That name, unless an age too late, or cold
Climat, or Years damp my intended wing.

When a man tells unprovoked lies about himself, you may reasonably infer that his emotions are seriously involved. Milton was not unskilled or unstudious of the literary artifice of the romances. By saying that he was, he betrays the deep feelings that made him turn against them. And the cause is that they are associated in his mind with his countrymen who have come so short of his standards. In both the prose and the verse passages quoted Milton blames the cold climate of England; in both occurs the scorn for mere toughness in war without balancing gifts of mind. Bitterly disillusioned in his patriotic fervour, Milton visits the sins of his countrymen on the whole tradition of the heroic poem.

Such is the reason I assign to Milton's dropping his historical poem. Why did he write *Paradise Lost*? If there is any one fact that should have emerged from this discussion it is that Milton had many literary projects in his mind. When he abandoned one, it was inevitable that the others should come to the fore. Let me recapitulate the literary themes or types, other than the heroic and patriotic, already mentioned as having been considered favourably by Milton, and add another not actually referred to by him but which he must have known and esteemed. First, there were the themes of Du Bartas: the Creation amplified with long scientific homilies, and Jewish history treated in a manner suggesting the writers of encyclopaedic world history. Second, there was the allegorical strain inherited from the Middle Ages. Of this there were clear signs in the plans for a tragedy in the Trinity

Manuscript. With the narrative allegory of man's pilgrimage Milton must have been familiar from the first two books of the *Faerie Queene*. There is yet another form of medieval allegory that Milton must have known: the warfare for the human soul. This theme can be close to that of the soul's pilgrimage, the difference being that of keeping or breaking the unity of place. Milton's chief authority for the Holy War would have been Phineas Fletcher's *Purple Island*. He does not mention the Fletchers, but there is sufficient evidence and an overwhelming *a priori* probability that he was very familiar with them. The *Purple Island* spends ten books on an elaborate allegory of the body and mind of man, and the last two on the warfare waged between the virtues and the vices for possession of them. The battle follows the scheme of the pilgrimage of man as narrated in the first book of the *Faerie Queene*. At the beginning the Intellect, governor of man, is able to resist the onslaught of evil by the forces at his disposal. But when Satan brings up all his powers, he is threatened with destruction. He is only saved by the intervention of Christ.

We shall never know by what reasoning, conscious or unconscious, Milton decided on the Fall as the subject of his epic. But we do know that he was able, in using that subject, to bring in all the themes or types mentioned above. He describes the Creation and includes the whole scope of world history. In Adam and Eve he could present Everyman and Everywoman, free from all suspicion of a now odious nationalism. And he can present them fought over by

Satan and Christ in the manner of Phineas Fletcher, and, at the end of the poem, setting out on their earthly quest for a mental paradise, in the manner of Spenser. Finally, he can now include what he had discarded. Having broken so completely with the heroic poem of the Renaissance in his main theme, he is free to include heroic matter in subordination. It is Satan who embodies some of the heroic qualities and who in his voyagings satisfies Milton's oft-repeated allusions to the *Odyssey* of Homer. It may even be that Milton modelled his plot on the *Odyssey*. Just as in the *Odyssey* the two large themes of Odysseus and Telemachus on their travels unite on Ithaca, so in *Paradise Lost* the forces of Heaven and Hell converge on Paradise for their supreme struggle. And as the motive of conflict narrows to the domestic struggle between Odysseus's family and Penelope's suitors, so the conflict in *Paradise Lost* is turned from the cosmic to the domestic. Thus it is that in the end Milton succeeded in uniting both his own multifarious projects and most of the epical strains—medieval and renaissance alike— that were alive in his own generation.

In one respect he went against his age. Near the time when *Paradise Lost* was forming in Milton's mind, two heroic poems were published, to which he was bound to pay attention: Davenant's *Gondibert* in 1651 and Cowley's *Davideis* in 1656. Though Milton probably agreed with almost the whole of the critical matter given in Davenant's admirable preface, he had no need to worry about the rhymed quatrains of *Gondibert* itself. He could see they were not destined to be the heroic measure of the future. But the couplets of the *Davideis* must have affected him otherwise. Here was a poem, the first original poem in English to affect the growingly fashionable neo-classic form in all its strictness and using the couplet in a new and vital way. Milton cannot have escaped the conviction that the couplet was the destined metre for the orthodox epic. I have no doubt that far from being serenely indifferent he was perturbed. Quite rightly he stuck to his own convictions, but I am certain he disliked going against the best contemporary practice. And both his perturbation and his dislike show themselves in the acrid tone of his note on the verse prefixed to *Paradise Lost*. Thus it was that even when he differed from his age, he was of it, in that he allowed full consideration to that very thing from which he was constrained to differ. *Paradise Lost* is remote from the *Lines at a Vacation Exercise*; yet both poems are alike in that they show not only the unique Milton but the Milton who lived, and moved, and had his being in the seventeenth century.

INDEX